Pioneer
Free Will Baptists
Ministers
Burial Locations
In
Ohio

To order additional copies of this book, contact:
FWB Publications
Enchanting Acres
1006 Rayme Drive
Columbus, Ohio 43207
Alton.loveless@prodigy.net
Or
www.amazon.com

FWB
FWB Publications

Introduction

Ohio

This book represents all that were part of the Free Will Baptist movement, consisting of the Palmer (south), Randall (north) and others such as the Stone, John-Thomas, John Wheeler Assns., NC OFWB and more.

Many of the photos are poor quality, but it was all I could find. Likewise, I do not have photos or tombstones for many of them. The information about these ministers were all that was available to me or found in archives. I made every effort to include those for which they would be remembered. Some I had no information, but research had shown they were of our denomination.

This State section was taken from the two Volume set by the same author.

Ohio

Walter Abrams
Birth:
1894
Death:
1979
Burial:
Lagrange Cemetery,
Ironton,
Lawrence County, Ohio

Rev Barton Davis Addis
Birth:
Jun. 2, 1866
Ohio
Death:
Oct. 3, 1916
Jamestown
Chautauqua County
New York
Burial:
Memorial Burial Park
Wheelersburg
Scioto County, Ohio

Portsmouth Daily Times
Portsmouth, Ohio
Saturday, 5 October 1916

REV. BARTON D. ADDIS
John P. Addis, of Harrisonville, former superintendent of the county infirmary, Wednesday afternoon received a telegram announcing the death of his brother, the Rev. Barton D. Addis, who had been living in Hyde Town, Pa. When relatives here last heard from Rev. Addis, he was enjoying splendid health. He was 50 years old last August and is survived by his wife and four children. His body left Hyde Town Thursday morning and will arrive here some time Friday.

Rev. Addis was a splendid minister and the news of his death will be learned of here with genuine sorrow. He was well known throughout Scioto County.

Portsmouth Daily Times
Portsmouth, Ohio
Saturday, 7 October 1916

FUNERAL NOTICE FOR REV. BARTON D. ADDIS
The funeral services of the late Rev. Barton D. Addis, who died in Jamestown, N.Y., will be conducted Sunday morning from the Glendale Church near Harrisonville. The body arrived here Friday and was conveyed to the home of the dead man's brother, John P. Addis of Harrisonville.

Portsmouth Daily Times
Portsmouth, Ohio
Monday, 16 October 1916

REV. BARTON D. ADDIS
Relative to the recent and sudden death of the late Rev. Barton D. Addis, a brother of John P. Addis, of Harrisonvile, the Titusville, Pa., Herald recently said: The many friends of Rev. B.D. Addis of this city and Hydetown were shocked to learn of his death in the W.C.A. hospital at Jamestown, N.Y., following an operation for gallstones performed earlier in the day.

Rev. Mr. Addis served the Hydetown M.E. Church the past year and at the Erie conference held two weeks ago in Clarion, he was assigned by Bishop Franklin Hamilton to the church at Sinclairville, N.Y., a thriving village about twelve miles north of Jamestown. He went to Sinclairville with his son, George Addis, in his automobile last Saturday. He preached both morning and evening Sunday and was taken ill soon after the evening service.

Being no better on Monday morning, the attending physician advised that he be taken to the Jamestown hospital and submit to an operation for gallstones. He was taken to the hospital on Monday afternoon and the operation was performed Tuesday morning.

Mrs. Addis was notified of her husband's serious illness on Monday evening and she went to Jamestown on the early New York Central train Tuesday, arriving at the hospital at 11 a.m., while Mr. Addis was still on the operating table. He rallied after the operation and knew his wife, but he gradually failed int he afternoon and passed away at 10 p.m.

Rev. Barton D. Addis had been a minister of the gospel for the past eighteen years and was 50 years, 4 months and 1 day of age. He was well known in Crawford County, where he had served numerous charges and during the past year, while in charge of the Hydetown pastorate had become acquainted with many residents of Titusville and vicinity. He was active in the tabernacle meetings held in this city last spring and conducted a series of evangelistic meetings in the Hydetown church following those services.

He leaves besides his wife, Mrs. Mary A. Addis, four children, George F., Wilbur J., Adra A. and Paul B. Addis, all of Hydetown, the eldest being a conductor on the Titusville traction line. He also has two brothers, John P. Addis, of Harrisonville, O., and George C. Addis, of Waterloo, O., and three sisters, Mrs. Millie Massie and the Misses Huttie and Bertha Addis, of Waterloo, O. He was a member of the Masonic Lodge at Pierpont, Ohio, and of the Hydetown I.O.O.F. Lodge.

Rev David Raymond Aiken
Birth:
June 28, 1946
Rosman, N.C.
Death::
April 29, 2020 (Age 73)
Edison, Ohio
Burial:
North Canaan Cemetery
Edison, Ohio.

Reverend David Raymond Aiken age 73, founder and president of the Central Ohio Association of Christian Broadcasters (COACB)

TV 39 and Parker-Hannifin retiree, died peacefully at home. David was an ordained Free Will Baptist minister and a pastor of numerous churches and a minister for over 50 years. Many people would recognize him as the host and pastor on the Word of Truth television program and pastor of the My Community Church.

David was born to Jesse and Thelma (Lowe) Aiken in Rosman, N.C.

David graduated from Pleasant High School in 1965. He enlisted in the army and pursued the field of critical communications. He was stationed in Germany for almost two years.

After being honorably discharged, David returned and married his long time sweetheart, Carolyn (Ratliff) Aiken.

David was one of the first squad members of the First Consolidated Volunteer Fire district in Caledonia, Ohio. David loved to travel and has been to all 50 states and multiple countries. David was passionate in his desire to build TV stations. He wanted to spread the gospel through television as far as he could. He built stations throughout central Ohio including stations in Marion, Columbus, Delaware, Ashland and Kenton. He helped others who had a similar desire by giving hands-on advice, equipment, and personal funds. His ministry was to reach out to others who needed Jesus Christ. A private funeral service for the family was with Dr. Freddy Dutton presiding. The service will be aired live on TV 39 and streamed on the COACB YouTube and Facebook.

Schuyler Aldrich
Birth:
Apr. 26, 1822
Ontario, Canada
Death:
Sep. 20, 1904
Buffalo, Erie County, New York
Burial:
Evergreen Cemetery, Pierpont, Ashtabula County, Ohio

He was brought to Christ in 1839, and studied at Oberlin College, Ohio receiving his ordination May 23, 1847. His ministry was with the Mecca, Henrietta, Pittsfield, and Macedonia churches, Ohio,

and with the Buffalo, Bethany, Phoenix, Elmira, and Poland churches, N. Y. Several revivals resulted from his labors, and about 200 converts were baptized by him. About 1880, he made his home in Buffalo, N. Y. His devotion to the cause of education is evidenced by a gift of ten thousand dollars to Hillsdale College, to be used in endowing a theological professorship.

Jonas Allen
Birth:
Royalton, Mass.
Death:
Sept. 29, 1864
Madison, Ohio
Burial:
Dock Road Cemetery Madison, Lake County, Ohio

Allen died aged 86 years. He was baptized by Elder Alva Buzzell, in 1809. At the close of the war of 1812 he began to preach, having his first revival in Charleston, Vt., where a church was organized, and he was ordained in 1824. Soon after churches were organized at East Charleston and at Brighton as a result of his labors. About 1837 he moved to Madison, Ohio, where he continued to preach until more than threescore and ten. He was devoted to every good work, enjoying the work of the ministry and awaiting in confidence for the rest prepared.

James Thornton Arthur
Birth:
Apr. 22, 1853
Pinkerman
Scioto County, Ohio
Death:
Oct. 14, 1925
Scioto County, Ohio
Burial:
Harrison Furnace Cemetery
Minford
Scioto County, Ohio

He was ordained on August 20, 1887 and spent several months in evangelistic work in the Little Scioto Quarterly Meeting in Ohio and then also in the Kentucky Yearly Meeting. At one time he pastored the Harrison church which is at Minford Ohio.

Leonard Ashley
Birth:
Jan. 19, 1792
Deerfield, Franklin County
Massachusetts
Death:
Jan. 31, 1873
Rockaway
Seneca County, Ohio
Burial:
Steuben Cemetery
Steuben, Huron County,Ohio

From the Biographical Record of the Counties of Huron and Lorain, Ohio. Chicago, J.H. Beers & Co. 1894 (305-306)
Leonard Ashley learned shoemaking under his father, and worked at the trade during his life in Massachusetts. His mother died about the year 1799, and the youth then went to reside with an elder brother, Luther. After some years he wished to see the world outside of his native State, and migrated to

Canada, where, in 1815, he married Sally McDougal, who was born in 1794, in Nova Scotia, for whose father young Ashley worked; and while living on Yonge street, and near Toronto, in the Province of Ontario, the following named children were born: Thomas, who died in infancy; James, who, in 1824, accompanied his mother to Ohio, where he married, became a Free-will Baptist preacher, and thence moved to Michigan, where he died, leaving twelve children ; Stewart B., late a resident of Steuben, Ohio, who died October 30, 1893, and is buried in Greenfield cemetery; Sally, who first married David Skeeles, and subsequently Dean Keefer (she is now a widow, residing at Columbus, Kans.); and John, a Free-will Baptist preacher, of Hillsdale, Mich., who was a fellow schoolmate of James A. Garfield. After the family joined the father in Greenfield township, in 1824, there were born Luther, a resident of Bellevue, Mich.; William, of Knoxville, Iowa; Allen T., the subject of this sketch; Joseph B., of Oberlin, Ohio; Mary, wife of Judge G. W. Lewis, of Medina, Ohio; Henry, a resident of San Francisco, Cal.; and Daniel, who went to California in 1862 and died there.

In 1822 Leonard Ashley left Canada for Huron County, Ohio, and worked on farms and at his trade here for two years. In 1824 his wife and children arrived, and all found a home with Alden Pierce, a brother-in-law, who then occupied what is known as the "Sturges Farm" in Greenfield Township. The father was known as a good farmer and a good shoemaker, and was a very active man until his death, which occurred in 1873. At that time he was on a visit to his son John at Rockaway, Seneca Co., Ohio, from which place his remains were returned to Huron County for interment in the Greenfield cemetery. His wife, who died March 19, 1863, was interred in Steuben cemetery. Leonard Ashley was a Whig until the organization of the Republicans, when he became a stanch supporter of the new party. In religious matters he and his wife were members of the Free-will Baptist Church."

Hobart C. Ashby
Birth:
Nov. 8, 1925
Virginia
Death:
Jan. 16, 1998
Dayton,
Montgomery County, Ohio
Burial:
Miami Valley Memory
Gardens,
Centerville,
Montgomery County, Ohio

He was ordained a Free Will Baptist minister in 1956. He began his pastoral duties in 1957 at the Fairborn Free Will Baptist Church where he served three years and in 1961, the Virginia born minister, became the pastor of the First Dayton Free Will Baptist Church, where he served for 33 years. Some 30 men answered the call to the ministry under his ministry. He retired from the church in 1994.

Rev Lewis A Atkinson
Birth:
Apr. 24, 1821
Virginia
Death:
Sep. 18, 1882
Jackson County, Ohio
Burial:
Fairmount Cemetery
Jackson
Jackson County,
Ohio

He was a minister of the Gospel. He served as a Captain in Co G 91st OVI in Civil War. Spouse: Amanda Long Atkinson (1832 - 1913). Children:
Charles Andrew Atkinson (1852 - 1925), Eliza Long Atkinson Strider (1856 - 1937), Mary Atkinson (1858 - 1859), Caroline Bundy Atkinson Jones (1866 - 1945).

He was a member of the Board of Directors of the Ohio State Association of Free Will Baptists for 22 years. Twice he was moderator of the Ohio State Association. He served six years on the national Home Missions Board. And preached at the national convention in Anaheim, California in 1980. He served in the U.S. Navy during WWII aboard the USS Crux in both the Atlantic and Pacific theaters.

Nehemiah Atwood
BIRTH
7 Dec 1792
Shenandoah County, Virginia, USA
DEATH
18 Dec 1869 (aged 77)
BURIAL
Calvary Baptist Cemetery
Rio Grande, Gallia County, Ohio

His parents were Sinnet ATWOOD and Letitia Grigsby Wood, ATWOOD, both bur. in Rileyville, Shenandoah Co. VA. He was a Sergeant in the 6th Regiment (Coleman's) VA Militia. He married Permelia Ridgeway, May 7, 1818, Gallia Co. OH. He is listed in this book because of the importance that he did in establishing a number of works in the state of Ohio then lastly with his wife, co-founder of Rio Grande College, Rio Grande, Ohio, which opened on September 13, 1876. Now the University of Rio Grande.

George Washington Baker
Birth:
Oct. 22, 1803
Litchfield Corners,
Kennebec County, Maine
Death:
Oct. 11, 1881
Marion, Marion County, Ohio
Burial:
Marion Cemetery,

Marion, Marion County, Ohio

One of the "Fathers" of the denomination in Ohio. He came from Litchfield, Maine, with his parents in 1822, and settled in Marion, Ohio until his death. He was converted under the labors of Rev. David Dudley and united with the Marion Free Will Baptist Church in 1827.

He received license to preach, though with the firm resolve that he would never be ordained. However, when his labors were crowned with success and he found himself surrounded by many converts who were pressing him to baptize them, he could refuse no longer, and in 1834, was ordained. He was pastor of churches, but he delighted in, and greatly preferred revival work. He was deeply spiritual, affectionate in manner, and a good singer. He was sustained by a large body and a strong constitution. He preached to all classes throughout the region. It is estimated that no less than 3,000 persons became professed Christians under his ministry, and 2,500 of these he baptized. Of these, some twenty-six entered the ministry. He continued to preach until the fall of 1880. During his long ministry, he took a prominent place in the general state and denominational work.

His last sermon was preached August 28, 1881, at a reunion of the pastors and members of the Centreburgh church, one of the first he gathered.

Rev Alvin Bacon
Birth:
Unknown
Death:
Dec. 5, 1818
Burial:
Rochester Station Cemetery
Rochester
Lorain County, Ohio, USA

Inscription:
Aged 27yrs 5mos 27dys

Clifford H. Ball
Birth:
Unknown
Death:
Feb. 22, 2007
Kansas City,
Wyandotte County,
Kansas
Burial:
Forest Lawn Memorial
Gardens,
Columbus,
Franklin County, Ohio

Clifford died in Kansas City but was the former pastor at Trinity Free Will Baptist Church and Welch Avenue Free Will Baptist Churches in Columbus, Ohio. He was the current pastor of the Bethel Free Will Baptist Church in Kansas City at his death.

Mance Ball
Birth:
1901,
Death:
1967
Scioto County, Ohio
Burial:
South Webster
Cemetery,
South Webster,
Scioto County, Ohio

Early Free Will Baptist minister in southern Ohio

Vernie Bare
Birth:
Oct. 22, 1926
Death:
Dec. 1, 2006
Burial
Ohio Western Reserve
National Cemetery,
Rittman,
Medina County, Ohio, Plot:
Section 20 Plot 189

Pastor of the Rock of Ages FWB Church.

Peter Barnhart
Birth:
Sep. 22, 1897
Death:
Aug. 8, 1993
Burial:
Lawrence Furnace Cemetery,
Lawrence Furnace,
Lawrence County, Ohio

Free Will Baptist preacher in the early days in southern Ohio.

Alva Buzzell at Strafford, Vermont. in 1812. Five years later he moved to Rutland, Ohio, where he was one of the early Free Baptists. He was licensed in 1837 and ordained at Cheshire in 1849. His ministerial labors were with the churches of the Meigs Quarterly Meeting of which he was clerk as early as 1835, and with several in the Athens Q.M.

Selah Barrett
Birth:
1790
Stafford,
Tolland County,
Connecticut
Death: there my
Jul. 12, 1860
Rutland,
Meigs County, Ohio
Burial:
Miles Cemetery,
Rutland,
Meigs County, Ohio
Barrett was baptized by Elder

Selah Hibbard Barrett
Birth:
Feb. 24, 1822
Rutland, Meigs County, Ohio
Sep. 1, 1883
Rutland, Meigs County, Ohio
Burial:
Miles Cemetery,
Rutland, Meigs County, Ohio

Deprived of the advantages of the schools because of ill health, he devoted perseveringly to study at home and gained a knowledge of the branches usually taught in college and afterwards completed courses in law and medicine. He experienced forgiveness of sins in 1838, received license to preach in 1845, and was ordained in 1856 by the Meigs Q. M., his ministry being spent within its bounds. He devoted much time to literary labor, having been a frequent correspondent of the *Morning Star* and other periodicals nearly forty years, and prepared several pamphlets and books, among them *"Memoirs of Eminent Preachers of the Freewill Baptist Denomination,"* and a Autobiography of about 400 pages.

Daniel E. Bates
Birth:
Feb. 2, 1927
Norton, Wise County,
Virginia
Death:
Aug. 16, 2010
Ohio
Burial:
Oak Grove Memorial Park,
Lexington,
Richland County,
Ohio

Pastor of the Blooming Grove Free Will Baptist Church.

Samuel D. Bates
Birth:
Oct. 13, 1828
Oneida County, New York
Death:
Sep. 17, 1886
Marion,
Marion County, Ohio
Burial:
Marion Cemetery, Marion,
Marion County, Ohio,
Plot: Sharpless Sect. S43 L1

Samuel D. Bates, D.D, in the fall of 1834 moved to Ohio, and settled in Trumbull Co. Samuel was reared on a farm but received his education at Geauga Seminary, which became a part of Hillsdale College, Michigan. He began to teach school when he was 19 years old and in 1848-49 taught the school at which James A. Garfield, afterwards President of the United States, was a pupil. Garfield was three years Mr. Bates' junior, and was persuaded to attend Geauga, from which a friendship existed until President Garfield's tragic death. Of Mr. Bates, Garfield once said, "To him I owe more than to any other living man for what I am today." He continued to teach until he entered the ministry of the Free Will Baptist Church in 1851. The first six years were spent in Trumbull Co. Ohio. In 1857 he came to Marion to accept the charge of the FWB church in that city. He remained pastor of the local church without interruption until 1876, and during his ministry of 19 years built up a strong congregation. When he came to Marion, the Free Will Baptist worshipped in the old church located on Mt. Vernon Avenue, but through his energy and executive ability the church on East Center Street was built at a cost of $16,000, more than half of which was donated outside of the society. He also was connected with the erection of five other church edifices in the county. He organized the Grand Prairie Free Baptist Church, and was its pastor for nine years. He organized the Claridon Free Will Baptist Church during the winter of 1870-71, and assisted in building the first church of that denomination in the township. He was pastor of the Claridon Church for 15 years, ministering to the wants of his people until a few months prior to his death. Mr. Bates was zealous in the cause of education as well as religion. He was a trustee of Hillsdale College for 15 years. In 1872 he was elected president of Ridgeville (Indiana) College and so continued up to the time of his death. In June 1884, Ohio Central College, at Iberia, in recognition of his thorough learning and earnest work in behalf of education, conferred upon him the degree of Doctor of Divinity.

(Marion County, Ohio, 1907 History, Biography)

Ben Bird
Birth:
Sep. 1, 1907
Death:
May 11, 1990
Burial:
White Gravel Cemetery,
Minford,
Scioto County, Ohio

Brother Bird's ministry was in the southern part of Ohio.

Warner Beebe
Birth:
Feb. 1, 1808
Death:
Oct. 5, 1851
Burial:
Beebe Town Cemetery,
Beebetown,
Medina County, Ohio
He was born Canandaigua, Ontario, NY. By 1825, he was in Liverpool, Ohio, where he united with the Free Will Baptist Church. He was ordained to the gospel ministry in 1835. In 1850, he represented the Ohio Northern Yearly Meeting in the General Conference.

James Andrew Blair
Birth:
Oct. 10, 1928
Kentucky
Jun. 25, 2004
Crossville,
Cumberland County,
Tennessee
Burial:
Miami Memorial Park
Cemetery,
Covington, Miami County,
Ohio

He was a retired minister, a member of Williams Road Freewill Baptist Church and attended Crossville First Freewill Baptist. He pastored for more than 30 years in the

Ohio area and was the founder of Troy Freewill Baptist Church in Troy, OH. He truly loved taking care of his people in the church. He was also a U.S. Army veteran, having served our country during Korea.

Rev Payton Blackburn
Birth:
Feb. 21, 1924
Lawrence County,
Kentucky
Death:
Oct. 3, 1991
Columbus
Franklin County,
Ohio
Burial:
Obetz Cemetery,
Obetz
Franklin County, Ohio

Blackburn, died at age 67, member and former pastor of the Hillview Freewill Baptist Church and Brice Road Freewill Baptist Church.

Retired from David Davies Packing in Columbus, Ohio after 20 years. Veteran of WW II. Payton was married to Edna (Gullett) daughters, Carol Willadean (Homer) Brickey, Betty Jean (Clyde) Endicott; sons, Cecil Payton, Rev Bobby Joe.

Orvil Blake
Birth:
Apr. 8, 1824
Death:
Aug. 12, 1877
Burial:
Westlawn Cemetery
Mantua,
Portage County, Ohio
Plot: Sect A, row 07

Blake, a native of Cornwall, Conn., married in 1850, and two years later moved to Mantua, Ohio, where he lived, labored, and died. His conversion and early labors were with the larger Baptist body, but as they refused him ordination because of his Free Baptist views, he found a home with the latter. He assisted in gathering several churches, and, besides his pastoral work at Mantua, preached also at Brimfield, Troy, Maple Grove, Hiram Rapids and Chester. He was a grand man, loved by all, and his death, at the age of 53 years, was a great loss to the

Yearly Meeting. He had lectured on various topics, was correspondent of several journals, and had represented his county in the State Legislature.

John Leonard Blount, Sr
Birth:
Jul. 18, 1930 Ohio
Death:
Apr. 10, 2006 Wilmington, Clinton County, Ohio
Burial:
Morrow Cemetery Morrow, Warren County, Ohio

Blount was the pastor of Beech Grove Church of God that later became the Beech Grove Free Will Baptist Church. He served as pastor from 1988-2006. The last year Rev. Allen Kinard assisted him in his duties.

David Lee Boggs
BIRTH
July 17, 1951
Columbus, Ohio
DEATH
May 6, 2020
Columbus, Ohio
BURIAL
Concord Cemetery West, Grove City, Ohio

David was born again on December 6, 1959. David was passionate about pouring the Word of God into men's souls. God sent him many young men over the years that he studied with, mentored, loved, and challenged to serve the Lord with all their heart, soul, and mind. He entered into vocational ministry in 1975 and was a gifted, expository Preacher for 45 years. He loved Mission Work and was part of the teams that started 10 Baptist Churches in Mexico, He also had the fortune of traveling to Canada, Paraguay, and Argentina to teach and preach God's Word. The funeral service was at Heritage Free Will Baptist Church,

Columbus, OH 43207, Pastor Jason Boggs officiated along with Pastor Dr. Tim W. Stout.

Marvin Booth
Birth:
Unknown
Death:
Feb. 17, 2000
Columbus, Ohio
Burial:
Obetz Cemetery,
Obetz, Franklin County, Ohio,
Plot: Sect 23, lot 91, spc 1

He founded in 1966 the Friendly FWB church in Columbus and pastored it for 25 years. At the time of his death he was pastor of the Reese Community Church. A noted leader and respected minister. He was 65 at his death.

Charles R. Bowman
Birth:
Jun. 25, 1924
Ramsey,
Nelson County, Virginia
Death:
Apr. 7, 2008
Columbus,
Franklin County, Ohio
Burial:
Alton Cemetery,
Alton, Franklin County, Ohio

He served our country in the United States Army during the Second World War, and had lived in Columbus, Ohio since 1952. He attended Moody Bible Institute and Liberty University. Rev. Bowman was gloriously saved on March 16, 1952 at Old Memorial Hall in Columbus, Ohio, and began preaching in 1953 and would preach everywhere the doors were opened. Many people accepted Christ as their personal Savior under his ministry. He pastored the Westside FWB Church for 35 years, and faithfully served this church and congregation through 1987. He also pastored in Key West, FL for ten years.

While We In The Dust And The Shadows Wait

Rev James Darmin Boyd

Birth:
Nov. 17, 1944
Logan
Logan County, West Virginia
Death:
Dec. 14, 2015
Mount Sterling
Madison County, Ohio
Burial:
Sunset Cemetery
Galloway
Franklin County, Ohio

He was a retired banker and served our country and protected our freedom by serving with the U.S. Navy as a Naval Hospital Corpsman with the U.S. Marine Corps. He was an ordained minister and a member of the Westside Freewill Baptist Church. His favorite saying was, "I preach the gospel for a living and work at a bank to support it." While living in Columbus, OH he served his community as a past president of the Hilltop Kiwanis and past President of the Hilltop Business Association. He served in numerous leadership positions with the Central Ohio Council of the Boy Scouts of America.

Rev Daniel Brackett

Birth:
Oct. 4, 1803
Berwick
York County
Maine
Death:
Dec. 22, 1836
Burial:
Old Ricker Family Cemetery
Locust Corner
Clermont County, Ohio

He was ordained a Free Will Baptist minister in 1829. He was residing in Houlton, and a council travelled over a hundred miles through the wilderness to ordain him. He labored in Maine, then journeyed to Ohio for his health and died of consumption at age 33.

Rev Hiram Brooks

Birth:
Apr. 23, 1810
Schoharie County, New York
Death:
Sep. 11, 1846
Ann Arbor
Washtenaw County, Michigan
Burial:
Bennetts Corners Cemetery
Brunswick
Medina County, Ohio,

Hiram Brooks was born 23 Apr 1810 in Schoharie County, New York, USA to

James and Lydia (Bennett) Brooks. Hiram must have initially come west with his family as evidenced by the following:

A Society of Free Will Baptists was organized in Bennett's Corners as early as 1828 with Hiram Brooks acting as lay minister." (From: Brunswick: Our Hometown A history of the community and its families)

The first school house was a log structure, erected in 1828, and located at the township corner-stone. Hiram Brooks was the first teacher, receiving $13.00 per month for his services, and boarding at home." (From the History of Medina County, page 593). It would appear that Hiram must have returned to the east to receive his theological training (possibly at either New Hampton Institute or Parsonsfield Seminary—not confirmed which one yet).

Hiram married Sarah Jane Hackett (daughter of Moulton and Mary (Ward) Hackett) 4 Dec 1839 in North Providence, Rhode Island, USA.

That same year Smithville Seminary was founded by the Rhode Island Association of Free Baptists. At the time, the Free Baptists already had two academies, one in New Hampshire (the New Hampton Institute), the other in Maine (Parsonsfield Seminary), and Rhode Island desired to have one of their own. Reverend Hiram Brooks was asked to start the school, and raised $20,000, all of which he put toward buildings. Sadly, the entire commitment of these monies to brick and mortar rather than an endowment fund may have caused financial difficulties for the institution, as it was unable to support itself through tuition revenue.

According to the History of Medina County, "One of the best saw-mills ever in Brunswick was built in the northeast part in 1843 by Hiram Brooks". "Hiram Brooks operated the mill until his death, which occurred some three years after its erection."

"This young man was a fine scholar, a graduate of one of the Eastern theological colleges, and often preached in cabins and schoolhouses in those early years. He had great resolution and superior courage."

The following notice of his death is from the: Free Baptist Cyclopedia, Historical and Biographical: The Rise of the Freewill Baptist Connection and of Those General and Open

Communion Baptists Which, Merging Together, Form One People, Their Doctrines, Polity, Publications, Schools and Missions, with Brief Biographies of Ministers and Others Identified with the Growth and Strength of the Denomination - 1889 By Rev G A Burgess and Rev J T Ward. Brooks, Rev. Hiram, died near Ann Arbor, Michigan, 11 Sep 1846, aged 36 years. His early labors were in Rhode Island where he assisted in raising funds for the school at North Scituate. He moved from La Grange, Lorain, Ohio to Michigan and was ordained but a little while before his death. He was well prepared for the ministry, and high hopes were entertained of his usefulness.

From records we believe that his son George H Brooks was born in New Jersey and daughters Sarah and Lucinda Jenny were born in Ohio. We also know that Sarah Jane, daughters Sarah F and Lucinda Jenny died in Lowell, Massachusetts. It is unknown whether his son, George H Brooks, died elsewhere or in Lowell, Massachusetts. No death record has been found. Aged 36y; ordained Freewill Baptist minister with great promise; sad he had to leave so soon.

Homer S. Brooks

Birth:
Feb. 9, 1926
Harrogate,
Claiborne County,
Tennessee
Death:
Feb. 11, 2003
Springfield,
Clark County, Ohio
Burial:
Ferncliff Cemetery,
Springfield,
Clark County, Ohio

Rev. Brooks was in the ministry for 54 years. He pastored the South Charleston Church for 35 years. In addition, he pastored the Sunset Church in Springfield for 18 years. For much of his ministry, while he pastored, he would preach 26 weeks of revivals for other churches. He was well known as an evangelist across the region. Brother Homer also was active in denominational roles, holding offices in the Little Miami Conference.

Rev Elias P. Brown

Birth:
Apr. 17, 1792
Strafford
Orange County
Vermont
Death:
Aug. 29, 1867

Ohio
Burial:
Cleveland Street Cemetery
Amherst
Lorain County, Ohio

Rev. Elias P. Brown, a native of Strafford, VT, died in Amherst, OH, aged 75 years. He was converted in youth, and joined the Free Baptists in Bethany, NY, where his labors were blessed. Later he moved to Lorain County, O., where he was ordained Nov. 10, 1836, and continued to preach until called to his reward. His birth is recorded in VT Vital Records and gives his father's name, and his mother, "Mary." Census' show his spouse as Mabel Brown. She is bur. in this cemetery.

Morgan Hillman Brown
Birth:
Feb. 16, 1901
Death:
Mar. 8, 1986
Burial:
Vernon Cemetery,
Lyra,
Scioto County,
Ohio

William Brundige
Birth: 1741
New York
Death: Nov. 12, 1825
Ohio
Burial:
Wyatt Cemetery
Waldo
Marion County,
Ohio

William BRUNDIGE was born in the vicinity of Rye, New York. He was the son of Joseph BRUNDIGE and Elizabeth JENNINGS Brundige.

On 29 October 1761 at Rye, New York, William Brundige married Anna PURDY.

William Brundige served in the Revolutionary War while living in New York.

Through the years, he was a Baptist minister in New York, Virginia, and Ohio.

William Brundige and Anna Purdy Brundige were among the first settlers of Waldo, Marion County, Ohio.

William Brundige died as reached the age of 84 years.

William Brundige (1741 - 1825) and his wife Anna

Purdy Brundige (1743 - 1823) are buried in historic Wyatt Cemetery near Waldo, Marion County, Ohio. Their children:

Anna Brundige Wyatt (1762 - 1838)*

Nathaniel Brundige (1771 - 1825)*

Sarah Nancy Brundige Tarboss (1773 - 1845)*

Thomas Brundige (1778 - 1844)*

John Brundige (1788 - 1850)*

Rev. Calvert was a member of the Beatty Freewill Baptist Church and was an avid fisherman. He was bi-vocational and was retired form Navistar.

Paul Russell Calvert
Birth:
Sep. 26, 1932
Yellow Springs,
Greene County, Ohio,
Death:
Mar. 11, 2010 Springfield,
Clark County, Ohio,
Burial:
Garlough Cemetery,
Pitchin,Clark County, Ohio,

Rev John Cannan
BIRTH
1789
DEATH
24 Nov 1848 (aged 58–59)
Ohio, USA
BURIAL
Pittsfield East Cemetery
Pittsfield, Lorain County,
Ohio

Albert N Carmine
Birth:
1879
Death:
1964
Burial:
Green Camp Cemetery
Green Camp
Marion County Ohio

He was on the 37th session program in 1907 Central Ohio Yearly Meeting at the west Mansfield FWB Church. He led in the Young People's Meeting as president.

Hamilton James Carr
Birth:
1810
New York
Death:

Apr. 8, 1887
Jackson, Jackson County, Ohio
Burial:
Fairmount Cemetery, Jackson, Jackson County, hio

He was the son of Walter Moore Carr. His first wife Rebecca Conaway died in 1845 in Alexander Twp., Ohio. After his wife and father died, he married Ziare and they moved to Jackson, Ohio, where he was a Free Will Baptist preacher until his death. He was pastor of several churches in the Ohio River Y. M. The first two years of his ministry he baptized over 200 persons. He organized many churches and aided in the ordination. of several ministers. He was one of the trustees and an earnest supporter of Rio Grande College. He represented Ohio at the 1880 Centennial Conference in New Hampshire and is pictured in the photo of those over the age of 70 at this meeting. He is in the front row right with Bible in his hand. He was active in his denomination. Mr. Carr was an anti-slavery man and a Republican. During Morgan's raid in Ohio he lost property and subjected to ill-treatment from the rebels.

John Casebolt
Birth:
1872
Death:
1959
Scioto County, Ohio
Burial
Bennett Cemetery,
Minford,
Scioto County, Ohio

A Righteous Child Has Great Joy.

Forrest L. Chamberlin
Birth:
Feb. 23, 1922
Scioto County, Ohio
Death:
Jun. 8, 2012
Portsmouth, Scioto County,
Ohio
Burial:
Vernon Cemetery,
Lyra, Scioto County, Ohio

Brother Chamberlin was one of the most respected ministers in southern Ohio. He was a retired barber and Free Will Baptist Minister ordained in 1947. He was the pastor of the Porter, Harrison, Long Run and Germany Hollow Free Will Baptist churches. However, his ministry extended beyond the local level and served on the Board of Directors for the Ohio State Association of Free Will Baptists for a number of years. He was active on various other committees and boards. He was a veteran of the United States Army serving during World War II in Germany and Austria as a radio operator with the 13th armored division.

Clarence O Clark
Birth: 1855
Death: 1943
Burial:
Calvary Baptist Cemetery,
Rio Grande,
Gallia County,
Ohio

He was a very active minister, pastor, leader and professor at Rio Grande College before and after the merger with the Northern Baptist.

Uriah Chabot
Birth:
Feb. 6, 1816
Greene, Ohio
Death
Aug. 18, 1897
Burial:
Powellsville Cemetery
Powellsville
Scioto County, Ohio

Rev Uriah Chabot was pastor in the early 1880s at "The Free Will Baptist "Church of Powellsville, Ohio. This church was originally organized on Aug 16, 1841, as nondenominational and it was the first church in Powellsville. In the early 1930's, it was organized as a Free Will Baptist Church. In 1884, Rev. Uriah Chabot was pastor at the Chaffin Mills FWB Church. Uriah Chabot was active in his community, not only as pastor, but in other areas as well. When the small Methodist Episcopal Church in Powellsville, was dropped out of circuit, Rev.

Uriah Chabot and Rev. Patrick Henry held a union meeting with them and it gave that church new life.

He married Luvina Hudson on 29 Sep 1841 in Scioto Co. and they had six children one of which was Dr. G. W. Shabot. He was converted the same year of his marriage and received license to preach in 1854 and was ordained in 1874 after which he became minister to many churches in the little Scioto and Pine Creek Quarterly Meetings.

Listed as a minister in the 1858 FWB Register from the Green Church.

Rufus B. Clark
Birth: Nov. 23, 1819
Conneaut,
Ashtabula County, Ohio
Death: Nov. 25, 1889

Conneaut
Ashtabula County, Ohio
Burial:
City Cemetery, Conneaut,
Ashtabula County, Ohio

Rufus was converted in 1830 and attended Geauga Seminary, and was ordained in 1843. For sixteen years he was pastor of the church in his native town, and he since ministered to the Lenox, Cherry Valley, Burgh Hill, New Lyme, Greenburg and Colebrook, Ohio; Sheffield and Wellsburg, Pennsylvania; Warren, Illinois, and Fon du Lac and Winneconne Wisconsin churches. He was actively identified with the anti-slavery movement. He was a life member of the Home and Foreign Mission Societies. He wrote sketches of the early history of Conneaut and other towns in northern Ohio. He delivered many lectures on various topics and a contributor to the religious and secular press. Rev. Clark wrote a *"Early History of South Ridge"*, about Ashtabula Co, in 1880.

Sam Crabtree
Birth:
Apr. 17, 1917
Otway, Scioto County, Ohio
Death:

Feb. 4, 1997
McDermott,
Scioto County,
Ohio
Burial:
Scioto Burial Park,
McDermott,
Scioto County,
Ohio

Bi-Vocational minister retired from the Empire-Detroit steel Corporation where he was stationary engineer. He was also a Free Will Baptist Minister for 47 years pastoring churches in the area.

Phillip E. Crabtree
Birth:
May 5, 1912
Death:
Jan. 14, 1994
Burial:
South Webster Cemetery
South Webster
Scioto County, Ohio

Phillip E. Crabtree, 81, of Oak Hill Branch Road, South Webster, died at a Columbus hospital. The son of the late John A. and Viola Lute Crabtree, he was a miner in a clay mine, a member of the Eifort Free Will Baptist Church, and a Free Will Baptist minister for 54 years. He is survived by his wife

Mallie Green Crabtree, who he married Oct. 31, 1932. He has a son who is a home missionary in New Brunswick, Canada.

Rev Claude T. Crain
BIRTH
3 Aug 1939
Wilder, Tennessee
DEATH
20 Jun 2019 (aged 79)
BURIAL
Dunkard Ridge Cemetery
Elmville, Highland County, Ohio

Reverend Claude T. Crain, age 79 of Huber Heights was born to the late Carl and Pauline Crain. In addition to his parents, Claude was preceded in death by his brothers: Clyde Crain and Calvin Crain. Claude was a Horticulturist

for the City of Dayton, and retired after 35 years of service. He was a minister in the Freewill Baptist Church; was a Sunday school teacher and deacon; and was a member of First Dayton Freewill Baptist Church. Claude and his wife devoted their lives to working for Christ and winning lost souls to Christ for the furtherance of His kingdom.

Cathy Dale Crawford
BIRTH
26 Jan 1952
Portsmouth,
Scioto County, Ohio
DEATH 9 May 2019
Portsmouth, Scioto County, Ohio,
BURIAL
Sunset Memorial Gardens
Franklin Furnace,
Scioto County,
Ohio

A daughter of the late Carl Edward and Georgie Mae Smith Crawford, Cathy was a 1970 graduate of Minford High School and attended Welch Bible College in Nashville, TN. She then spent 30 years as a missionary in France. Cathy enjoyed going to tea houses and preferred black tea. She was a faithful servant who loved the Lord and was loved by everyone she met.

Funeral services at WOLFE-NELSON FUNERAL HOME in Sciotoville with Pastor Mike Mounts officiating.

Ravenswood, W.Va. WW II Marine Veteran, serving when Pearl Harbor, Hawaii, was attacked in 1941. Life member Middleport DAV 53. he was a lifelong member of the Meigs County Free Will Baptist Association and a member of the General Board for the Ohio Association of Free Will Baptists.

William Ershel Curfman
Birth:
Aug. 8, 1920
Ohio
Death:
Feb. 7, 2000
Gallipolis, Gallia County, Ohio
Burial:
Gravel Hill Cemetery,
Cheshire,Gallia County, Ohio

Ordained October 6, 1951 by the Freewill Baptist Church. He pastored the following Freewill Baptist Churches: Kelly's Creek and Spring Hollow, West Virginia, Mt. Olive, Bidwell, Ohio, Coalton, Ohio, Old Kyger, Ohio. and Centerpoint, Ohio., where he was a member. Retired Blacksmith, Kaiser-Aluminum Plant,

Elial Curtis
Birth:
Connecticut
Death:
September 19, 1848
New Haven, Ohio
Burial:
Guinea Corners Cemetery
Huron County, Ohio

He was a native of Connecticut and in his early life moved to New York then later to Ohio. He was ordained in 1837 and died at New Haven. He was a judicious brother, safe in Counsel, careful in deportment, highly esteemed by a large circle of Christian friends.

Rev. Delmer Daniels
BIRTH
May 19, 1915
Offutt, Kentucky
DEATH
March 24, 1964
People's Hospital
Mansfield, Ohio
BURIAL
Mansfield Memorial Park
Mansfield, Ohio

Rev. Daniels was a member of the Northern Ohio Conference of Free Will Baptists and the Kentucky State Association of Free Will Baptist. He was the pastor of the Wyandotte Free Will Baptist Church and had lived in that vicinity for 14 years. He was 48 years old at his passing.

Rev John Andrew Daniels
Birth:
Sep. 20, 1928
Death:
Dec. 10, 2016
Burial:
Obetz Cemetery
Obetz
Franklin County, Ohio
Reverend John Andrew Daniels age 88 passed away peacefully at home. John was born to his parents, the late John H. and Roseanna Daniels in Patrick, Kentucky. He followed the call to minister for over 67 years. Retired from White Westinghouse Corp.
A member of The Mechanicsburg Freewill Baptist Church. Preceded in death by his wife of 54 years. Pastor Jesse Walters officiating.

Budd L. Darst
Birth:
1900
Gallia County, Ohio
Death:
1993
Gallia County, Ohio
Burial:
Gravel Hill Cemetery,
Cheshire, Gallia County, Ohio

Herbert C. Davis

Birth:
Mar. 21, 1934
Johnson County, Kentucky
Death:
Sep. 3, 2012
Fairborn, Greene County, Ohio
Burial:
Byron Cemetery, Fairborn, Greene County, Ohio

He was born in Johnson Co., Kentucky, the son of the late James Herbert and Alka (Sadler) Davis. Herb was employed with General Motors as a tool and die maker, retiring in 1982; and was a minister for over 50 years at many churches. One of Herb's hobbies was woodworking and enjoyed playing the violin and singing while Anna played the piano with him.

John Merrill Davis

Birth:
Nov. 16, 1846
Harrisonville, Meigs County, Ohio
Death:
Nov. 11, 1920
Raccoon Township, Gallia County, Ohio
Burial:
Calvary Baptist Cemetery, Rio Grande, Gallia County, Ohio

His childhood education was in the public schools of Scipio Township. He joined the Free Will Baptist denomination in 1860 and in 1863 served the Government as an army teamster during the Civil War. Between March and September of 1865 he served in active duty with the 188th Ohio Volunteer Infantry. He entered Ohio University in 1868 and graduated in 1873. He was ordained in 1872. In 1874, he became President of Ridgeville College in Indiana and pastor of the Free Will Baptist church there. In 1876 He received his M.A. from Ohio University and in 1878 took over Wilkesville Academy in Ohio 15 miles from Rio Grande College where he joined the college staff a year later.

In 1887 he became the third president of Rio Grande College at the age of 41. He served Rio Grande College for 40 years and 24 of those as President. He resigned as president in 1911, but remained on the faculty until 1919, also returning to ministerial duties. The University of Wooster conferred upon him the Ph.D. Degree. Ohio University conferred upon him the honorary degree of Doctor of Divinity. He served as President of the Southeastern Ohio Teacher's Association. President of the Ohio Free Communion Baptist Association. Delegate to several Free Baptist General Conferences between 1883 and 1904. Delegate to the Federal Council of Churches of Christ in Americas. He played an active role in the merger between Free Baptist and the Northern Baptist in 1911.

Alfred Franklin Delawder
Birth:
Jun. 4, 1878
Death:
Jun. 17, 1963,
Jackson County,
Ohio
Burial:
Glen Roy Cemetery,
Glen Roy,
Jackson County, Ohio

Early Free Will Baptist pastor in southern Ohio.

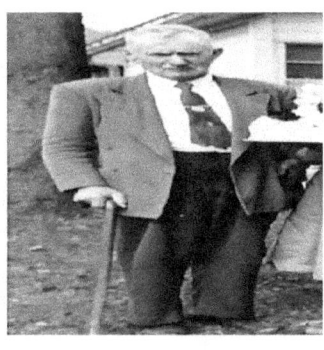

Rev Roy Tommy Depreist
Birth:
Sep. 29, 1931
Center Station
Lawrence County, Ohio
Death:
Jun. 4, 2014
Columbus
Franklin County, Ohio
Burial: Obetz Cemetery
Obetz
Franklin County, Ohio

Roy C. "Tommy" Depriest, to

Floyd and Nora Depriest who preceded him in death.

Roy trusted Christ as his Savior at a young age when his mother took him to Mount Calvary Baptist Church. He often spoke how he was baptized in the creek near that church. In 1953, Roy announced that God had called him to preach the gospel and was ordained as a Free Will Baptist minister and very faithful to that call till major issues caused he and his first wife to divorce.

Roy served in the US Navy during the Korean War. Following that, he returned to southern Ohio and got a job as a Safety Supervisor at Marquette Cement Company. He enjoyed reminiscing about a revival in 1958 when he, Calvin Evans, his cousin Eddie Depriest and another minister preached revival services at the Mt. Calvary FWBC near his birthplace. During those revival days, more than 150 people were won to Christ and baptized.

Roy liked to tell and show pictures of a special baptism service when they broke through 3 inches of ice and planned to baptize 29 people in the Ohio River. More were saved at the River and joined were also baptized. He testified that about 5,000 people were present!

After 25 years of service, Roy retired as Director of Manufacturing from Stewart and Warner in Chicago, IL. Roy and Doris faithfully attended Immanuel Lutheran Church (Crystal Lake, IL) for many years. In 1993, they returned to Ohio and were active members at a local Lutheran Church. Roy served that Church as a Deacon and Board Member.

In 2002, they returned to their Free Will Baptist roots and on March 2, 2003, they became members at Heritage FWBC..

Thomas Dimm
Birth:
1810
Pennsylvania
Death:
Jul. 10, 1886
Huron County, Ohio
Burial:
Guinea Corners Cemetery
Huron County, Ohio
A native of Pennsylvania, moved to Ohio in 1834, and

united with the Free Baptist Church in Huron, Ohio in 1841. He was ordained in 1844, and for several years labored in the Lake Erie Quarterly Meeting and subsequently with the Seneca, Huron and Lorain Quarterly Meetings. The last years of his life he was afflicted with blindness, but maintain his integrity and his love for Christ and the denomination he had served.

Eusebius M Dodge
Birth:
May 22, 1806
Lyme
New London County,
Connecticut
Death:
Jan. 2, 1852
New Lyme
Ashtabula County, Ohio
Burial:
Dodgeville Cemetery
New Lyme,
Ashtabula County, Ohio

An ordained Freewill Baptist minister from Ohio who was faithful in his service. Rev. Dodge, was the son of Eld. Eusebius and Anna (Merchant) Dodge--family records state that his father was also a Baptist clergyman, as well as Justice of the Peace. Eusebius M. married Hannah H. Hall, Oct. 15, 1826.His parents and extended families moved to Ohio where Rev. Eusebius was ordained as an evangelist, Oct. 15, 1837. He labored with poor churches and in destitute places, and saw many souls converted.He was a man of uncommon power, with great faith and perseverance and love for people. He baptized about a thousand persons.He died at an early age of 45 years.

He moved from Conn., in 1811, along with ninety persons from Conn., (per local records), through great privations and hardships on the trip in the wilderness and terrain, to Ohio, where he and his family established themselves in the new country. He bought 1,200 acres of land, and became a representative citizen, taking part in community affairs, and business, where they lived. He owned a mercantile business at one time, hauling supplies from Pittsburg by oxen.

Eusebius served in the 1812 Spanish Amer. War, and his father, Jeremiah, served in the American Revolution (DAR records).

He married Anna Merchant, 02 Feb. 1794, Lyme Co. CT., (CT mar. records). They raised ten children, many bur. in this cemetery. Three sons, John, Calvin, and Hiram L; daughters,

Cyrus Dudley
Birth:
Unknown
Death:
Mar. 3, 1871
Blanchester, Ohio
Burial:
West Woodville Cemetery
Warren County, Ohio

His parents were Peter DUDLEY and Ruby (Soule) DUDLEY. He married Frances Teetor, 1819. They had three children: Hannah, Colmbus J., and Amelia E. There were several "Dudley" families from Maine who migrated to Ohio and began the town, "Maineville," because so many from Maine had come. Rev. Cyrus Dudley, a native of Maine, died at the age of 70 years. When quite young he became a member of the Maineville Freewill Baptist Ohio church. He was married and settled in West Woodville, where he resided until his death. In 1835 he commenced his ministerial duties and until near the close of life was active in the work. He was a man of much power in the pulpit, and successful as an evangelist.

David Dudley
Birth: Jul. 16, 1791
Mt Vernon, Maine
Death: May 29, 1867
Waldo, OH
Burial:
Wyatt Cemetery,
Waldo, Marion County, Ohio

He was an early Free Will Baptist Minister, first found in the Ohio records at Rutland, Ohio. He attended the General Conference at Mainsville, Ohio, where he later pastored. However, most of his ministry was to be found in Marion County, Ohio, where many of his churches still exist. He had a powerful influence during his early days in Ohio, but for a while he ministered in Iowa where his first wife died. He returns back to Ohio and here married Lovinah Wyatt. He was the 2nd husband of Lovinah Brundige Wyatt, widow of Samuel Wyatt.
Source: "Ohio, the cross road of our nation", Vol IV, No. IV.

Moses Dudley
Birth:
1755 Maine
Death:
Nov. 24, 1842
Maineville, Warren County, Ohio
Burial:
Maineville Cemetery,
Maineville, Warren County, Ohio
In 1815, Moses Dudley, with his family, moved from Maine and settled in Maineville.

Dudley built the first frame house in the village. The Maineville Free-Will Baptist Church was organized by Elder Moses Dudley, Henry Greely and others as early as 1822 or 1823. It was called Salt Spring Church. For a number of years they worshiped in a schoolhouse east of Maineville, and not far from the Maineville Graveyard. About 1830, they built the present brick building. Elder Moses Dudley was the first pastor of this church.

ME, where he remained until his removal to Ohio, about 1853, or seven years before his death.

Charles Thomas Dutton
Birth:
Jan. 15, 1927
Dickerson County, Virginia
Death:
Jan. 12, 2004
Marion,
Marion County, Ohio
Burial:
Grand Prairie Cemetery,
Brush Ridge,
Marion County, Ohio

Thomas Dudley
Birth:
Apr. 18, 1783
Mount Vernon,
Kennebec County, Maine
Death:
Aug. 7, 1860
Pagetown,
Morrow County, Ohio
Burial:
Crossroads Cemetery,
Albany, Athens County, Ohio

He was the brother of Rev. Moses Dudley, who moved to Ohio and died in Warren, Ohio, and buried in Maineville Cem. At the age of eighteen he joined the church in Mt. Vernon, ME where he was ordained about 1813. In 1836, he moved to Pittsfield

He was a longtime Free Will Baptist Minister serving in the northern Ohio Association.

Jimmy R Dutton
Birth:
Jul. 20, 1940
Clintwood VA.
Death:
Aug. 22, 2014
Burial:
Grand Prairie Cemetery
Brush Ridge
Marion County, Ohio

He was born to the late Ervie and Keturia (Fletcher) Dutton.
He was preceded in death by his first wife, June (Taylor) Dutton; survived by his second wife, Mildred (Becky)

Holt Dutton. Jimmy retired in 2002 after working for Khempco Building Supply.
Jimmy loved the Lord and preached the gospel for many years leading people to Christ, living life to it's fullest always putting God first. He enjoyed his bluegrass music. He started playing fiddle at age 16. He could play many instruments, but his favorite was the mandolin and fiddle. He had a bluegrass gospel program called HYMNTIME that aired on the local TV station in Marion for almost 20 years. He has played music in his own bands; The Dutton Brothers, Kentucky Grass and New Gospel Ship. He has played with Red Allen, Kenny Baker, and Lillie Mae and the Dixie Gospel Aires. He also enjoyed photography especially stills like flowers and collecting cameras. Pastor Grover Caudill officiated assisted by Rev. Freddie Dutton.

Joseph EATON

Bathsheba Sackett Eaton
Birth
10 Dec 1766
Pennsylvania
Death
26 Dec 1838
Delaware County, Ohio
Burial
Townhouse
Cemetery
Lewis Center, Delaware
County, Ohio

Joseph Eaton
Birth
1766
Huntingdon Pa
Death
8 Feb 1825
Burial
Cheshire Cemetery
Delaware, Delaware County,
Ohio
Plot; Located in old
Townhouse Cemetery, is in
rear section of Cheshire
Cemetery

Wife of Joseph Eaton and mother of Mary (Eaton) Cunningham, David Eaton, Joseph Eaton, Elizabeth (Eaton) Wilson, Rev. Isaac Eaton, Rev. James Eaton, Rachael (Eaton) Crawford, and Rev. George Eaton.

Wife of Joseph Eaton and mother of Mary (Eaton) Cunningham, David Eaton, Joseph Eaton, Elizabeth (Eaton) Wilson, Rev. Isaac Eaton, Rev. James Eaton, Rachael (Eaton) Crawford, and Rev. George Eaton.

Revolutionary War veteran. Immigrated to Ohio from Pennsylvania in 1805. born son of David Eaton and grandson of Rev Joseph Eaton and Gwenllian Morgan issued 12 children removed to Ohio in 1808 with the Johnston family , founder of Eatonville Ohio.

Clark officiating.
Burial followed where military graveside rites were performed by the William A. Baker and James Irwin Posts of the American Legion. (Portsmouth Daily Times, March 6, 2013)

Donald Enos Ellis
Birth:
Mar. 20, 1931
McDermott, Scioto County, Ohio
Death:
Mar. 4, 2013
Portsmouth, Scioto County, Ohio
Burial:
Rush Township
Scioto County, Ohio

He was born a son of the late Charles and Lula Mae Kennard Ellis. Don was a retired mechanic from Dayton Walther Corp, Pastor of Stoney Run Free Will Baptist Church, and a U.S. Navy Veteran. Funeral services were conducted at the Stoney Run Freewill Baptist Church with Craddock Frye and Roger

John Elswick
Birth:
1891
Death:
1947
Scioto County, Ohio
Burial:
Buckeye Cemetery,
Ohio Furnace,
Scioto County, Ohio

John William Elswick
Birth:
Jul. 27, 1938
Lawrence County, Kentucky
Death:
Jul. 26, 2006
Columbus, Franklin County, Ohio
Burial:
Graham Chapel Cemetery,
Athens County, Ohio

He was the son of the late Fred and Malissia Ellen Boggs Elswick. He was a 1957 graduate of Shade High School. He was retired from Ohio University after 31 years. He was also a minister for the past 38 years. He was recently the pastor of the Carpenter Baptist Church and Poplar Ridge Free Will Baptist Church. He was a member of Grahams Chapel Church. He was involved with the World Christian Outreach Ministry with Rev. Dr. David T. Rahamut.

Quentin U. England
Birth:
Unknown
Death:
Mar. 30, 2000
Burial:
Obetz Cemetery,
Obetz,
Franklin County,
Ohio,
Plot: Sect 25, lot 34, spc 1

He was active in the early organization of the Ohio Free Will Baptist Association. He was a member of the Franklin Conference where most of his ministry was.

Floyd J. Estep
Birth:
Jan. 6, 1911
Paintsville,
Johnson County, Kentucky
Death:
Feb. 6, 2009
Portsmouth,
Scioto County, Ohio
Burial:
Evergreen Union Cemetery,
Waverly Pike County, Ohio

He was a member of the Wakefield Free Will Baptist Church, a retired N W Railroad employee, an active Free Will Baptist Clergyman, former pastor of seven Free Will Baptist Churches, Member of Lucasville, Ohio. Life Certificate in Scioto Ministerial Conference of Free Will Baptist and Veteran of WWII.

Calvin Evans
Birth:
Mar. 30, 1930
Death:

Jan. 11, 2006
Tampa,
Hillsborough County,
Florida
Burial:
Highland Memorial Gardens,
South Point,
Lawrence County, Ohio

He was nationally known for founding the Evangelistic Outreach Inc. 48 years ago with a $250 love offering. It grew to spread the word through the Internet, a weekly television show and a daily radio show in numerous markets in the tri-state and throughout the Midwest. He was well-known for his revivals, one of which lasted 13 weeks. Evans started the Spring Jubilee which is held every spring at the Scioto County Fairgrounds. He had worldwide crusades in decade in Jamaica, Uganda and Haiti. He had extended ministries in many countries in the Caribbean. He had thousands to complete correspondence courses in his outreach efforts. Evans, 75, had just entered his fifth decade as an evangelist. He preached his first sermon in 1956 and pastored in churches in Ohio and Kentucky. He was ordained by the Free Will Baptist Denomination and had preached in the national convention in 1974 in Wichita, Kansas to 5000.

Fred C Evans

Birth: Aug. 7, 1926
Blaine,
Kentucky
Death: Nov. 26, 2001
Burial:
Galena Cemetery,
Galena,
Delaware County, Ohio

Rev. Evans was the second pastor of the Welch Avenue Free Will Baptist Church in Columbus, Ohio. He served as Pastor from January 1958 through March 1961 when he left to serve for many years at the Pleasant View Free Will Baptist Church. Afterwards, he began the Greenleaf Road Free Will Baptist Church, which today is called the Southwest Free Will Baptist Church. At the time of his passing, he was 75 years of age and had completed over

52 years in the ministry.

He was pastor of the Faith Harvest Church in Marysville, Ohio at the time of his departure. The funeral services were conducted by Rev. Paul Thompson and the Rev. Glenn Derifield. He was also a veteran of the US Navy serving during WW II.

Vernal Lee Fairchild
Birth:
Jun. 14, 1928
Blaze,
Morgan County, Kentucky
Death:
Sep. 1, 2011
Xenia,
Greene County, Ohio
Burial:
Valley View Memorial Gardens,
Xenia,
Greene County,,Ohio

Rev. Fairchild was a graduate of Bethany Bible College where he received his Bachelor of Ministry degree.

He also graduated from ITT Technical Institute.

He was the Retired Pastor of Fellowship Tabernacle in Xenia; formerly Pastor of Sunset Freewill Baptist Church in Springfield and served as a chaplain with Greene Memorial Hospital. He began his ministry as Director of Xenia Rescue Mission and retired from Wright Patterson Air Force Base.

Edmund Burke Fairfield
Birth:
Aug. 7, 1821
Virginia
Death:
Nov. 17, 1904
Oberlin, Lorain County, Ohio
Burial:
Westwood Cemetery
Oberlin, Lorain County, Ohio
Plot: O-10

Rev. Dr. Edmund Burke

Fairfield Theologian, Educator, Politician and Author. Rev. Fairfield was born in Parkersburg, Virginia which at present is Parkersburg, West Virginia. He was a graduate of Oberlin College in 1842. Studied theology for three years while teaching school after graduation. Received an honorary LL.D. degree from Madison University (now Colgate University), a D.D. degree from Indiana University and the Sacrae Theologiae Doctor (Doctor of Sacred Theology) from Denison University. After two years of ministry he then accepted the Presidency of Michigan Central College (later known as Hillsdale College) in 1848. He held the position for twenty-one years. His political ambitions also came into play from the years 1857-1861. During this time he was elected to the Michigan Senate (1857-1858) and as the 12th Lieutenant-Governor of Michigan (1859-1861). Rev. Fairfield's reputation began to grow after his powerful speech on the Prohibition of Slavery in the Territories. It has been said that 50,000 copies of the speech were published and distributed. In 1864, after a ten month tour in Europe, Rev. Fairfield started a series of lectures which ran through fifteen states. In the anti-slavery and war campaign he took a prominent part in Michigan, Ohio and Indiana. He was later elected the second Chancellor of the University of Nebraska in 1876. He held this position for six years. The last term of administration was one of the most heated times in the history of the university. Rev. Fairfield was a Fundamentalist Christian and strongly opposed the teaching of Darwinism. On his faculty were three young professors who were attempting to bring Modernism to the young university. Some accounts say Rev. Fairfield was later forced to leave his position. In actuality, he and all the other professors resigned in 1882. After his resignation he again assumed pastoral duties until 1889. At this time he accepted the position of United States consul at Lyons, France having been appointed by President Benjamin Harrison. He held the position for four years. The Rev. Dr. Edmund Burke Fairfield retired from active public life to Oberlin, Ohio in 1900.

His Parents were Micaiah Fairfield (1786 - 1858) & Hannah W. Fairfield (1787

Raymond Lewis Fife

Birth:
Apr. 29, 1937
Meigs County
Ohio

Death:
Nov. 2, 1993
Point Pleasant
Mason County, West Virginia
Burial:
Gravel Hill Cemetery
Cheshire, Gallia County, Ohio

Minister in SE Ohio. Parents: Albert Raymond Fife and Anna Myrtle Ward. Wife: Anita Ann Scott

Anthony Franklin

Birth:
Feb. 11, 1968
Delaware
Delaware County, Ohio
Death:
Dec. 15, 2014
Chesterville
Morrow County, Ohio
Burial:
Maple Grove Cemetery
Chesterville
Morrow County, Ohio

He was born, the son of Paul I. and Ida Christeen (VanHoose) Franklin, in Delaware, Ohio. Tony grew up in Ashley and graduated from Buckeye Valley High School in the class of 1986, where he enjoyed playing football and basketball.

On August 10, 1991, Tony married Jerri I. McDaniel in Lewis Center, Ohio. Together they shared 23 wonderful years of marriage.

Tony he enjoyed working for Delaware Hayes High School where he was a teacher's aid in the multiple handicap classroom. He also enjoyed sharing God's word as a preacher at the North Woodbury Freewill Baptist Church.

Tony had a strong faith in the Lord and loved going to church and various church related activities such as camps and plays.

Two years before his passing, Tony was diagnosed with stage 4 colon cancer. That is where his faith and trust was really put to the test. With all of the struggles he had, he never complained and always kept a smile on his face because he knew God had him under His wings and was taking care of him.

Kenneth Lee Frisbee, Sr
Birth:
Dec. 25, 1928
Marion, N.C.
Death:
Oct. 21, 2017
Burial:
Hillside Memorial Park
Akron
Summit County
Ohio,

Pastor Kenneth Lee Frisbee, Sr., faithfully served the Lord Jesus Christ from age 19 until his passing at 88.. He was born to parents, Roy and Mae (Maney) Frisbee.

He is survived by his loving family: wife, Betty; sons, Kenneth Lee Frisbee Jr. (Nancy) of Marion, N.C. and Dennis Wayne Frisbee (Lois) of Brimfield, Ohio; brothers, Cecil, Bruce, and Bobby; sisters, Ruby (deceased), Ruth, Betty Jo, and Sandra; seven grandchildren, Kenny III (Laura) and Todd (Lesley) of California, Megan and John of Marion, N.C., Sheila (David) of Green, Roy (Kerri) and David (Kelly) of Tallmadge; and fourteen great-grandchildren;

He also leaves his church family which he pastored for 57 years, friends who fondly remember his love and concern for them all.

Isaac Fullerton, Sr
Birth:
Feb. 15, 1809
Greenbrier County,
West Virginia
Death:
Nov. 11, 1886
Scioto County,
Ohio
Burial:
Butler & Martin Cemetery,
Minford,
Scioto County
Ohio

He moved with his parents while still young and settled in Scioto Co., Porter Township, Ohio. He and his sons entered the War in 1861...Rev. Isaac was a Capt. in 59th OH. Rev. Rufus Cheney was the first preacher of the denomination to preach in Scioto Co., in 1816, and he organized the Porter Free Will Baptist Church Sept. 6, 1817, in a schoolhouse on Ward's Run. Rev. Fullerton received license to preach in 1834, and was ordained to the gospel ministry in November 1836. He farmed to provide for his growing family, and most of his long ministry (about 52 yrs) was spent with the FWB churches of Little Scioto Quarterly Meeting, where he had been closely identified with all its work, organizing the FWB church in Wheelersburg, May 17, 1851, and was first pastor of the Sciotoville Church. He attended the General Conference at Marion (1886) as a delegate from the Ohio and Kentucky Y.M.

(Info from Ohio records, family genealogy, and Hist. of Ohio, 1884, chap 17, in archives).

Rev Samuel Fulton
Birth:
Aug. 10, 1856
Gallia County
Ohio
Death:
Mar. 23, 1912
Springfield Township
Gallia County
Ohio
Burial:
Gravel Hill Cemetery
Cheshire
Gallia County, Ohio

Rev. Samuel Fulton, a well-known and highly esteemed F. B. minister, died at his home in Bidwell Sunday evening, after long and brave struggle with asthma and lung trouble.

He had been living at Brunswick, O., and the last few years where he was engaged in the ministry, but was compelled on account of failing health to give up regular pastoral work several months ago. Realizing his time on earth was short he expressed a desire to spend his last days near relatives and friends, and with his family moved to Bidwell only a few weeks ago.

The last sad rights were held at the Campaign Church. Conducted by Rev. J. M. Davis of Rio Grande, Samuel Fulton, son of Samuel and Nancy Malaby Fulton, being 55 years, seven months and 14 days old. He suffered a lingering sickness, after being ill since August 1911. He was fully conscience of his condition and said many times he was coming to what lies ahead of us all.

He was united in marriage March 28, 1876 to Elizabeth Shuler. To this union six children were born. The oldest to precede him, and four survive him as follows: one son Wm. Fulton, of Morral, Ohio, Mrs. Hugh Quinn, of Huntington, W. Va., Mrs. Leo Barry, of Morral Ohio, and Miss Petal at home, and with their sorrowing mother mourn his departure. He also leaves three brothers, Royal of Kansas, W.J. of Rio Grande, and J. of Gallipolis, and one sister Mrs. Mary E. Pierce, of Iowa.

Inscription:
FULTON
REV

SAMUEL FULTON
1856 - 1912
ELIZABETH FULTON
1855 - 1948
SWEETLY RESTING

Rev. Samuel Fulton was a brother of Rev. W. J. Fulton, also a Free Baptist minister.

William J Fulton
Birth:
1847
Death:
1927
Burial:
Calvary Baptist Cemetery, Rio Grande, Gallia County, Ohio
Rev. Dr. Wm. Fulton pastored Calvary FWB Church for 40 years, and was teacher in Rio Grande College. He was one of the most popular and respected ministers in Southeast Ohio and especially after the death of Rev. Ira Haning. He died at 80 yrs.

Millard Green

Birth:
1917
Death:
2001
Burial:
Burbank Cemetery
Burbank
Wayne County, Ohio

He was pastor of the Creston church for many years in northern Ohio.

Rev Cornelia Evangeline White Gow
Birth:
Nov. 4, 1860
Scioto County
Ohio
Death:
Aug. 28, 1950
Parkersburg
Wood County
West Virginia
Burial:
Radnor Cemetery
Radnor
Delaware County
Ohio

Retired Minister, of Pomeroy Pike, Belpre, Ohio. Daughter of Horace & Mary Eliza

(Pinkerman) White, Cornelia was married to Rev. David William Gow on February 18, 1879. They were the parents of three children: Rev. Ruda Marion, William Purvis, and Lillian Minerva.

Rev David William Gow
Birth:
Aug. 7, 1859
Scioto County, Ohio
Death:
Jul. 12, 1938
Lima
Allen County
Ohio
Burial:
Radnor Cemetery
Radnor
Delaware County, Ohio
Baptist Minister, of North Pearl Street, Spencerville, Ohio. At the time of his death he was the oldest active minister in point of service in the state. His last charges were at Needmore and Neptune.

He was the son of William Purves Gow, a native of Scotland, and Mary Ann Brown, of Scioto County, Ohio. He was converted at the age of 14 years. At the age of 19 he began work in the ministry. February 18, 1879, he was united in marriage to Cornelia E. White of Scioto County. To this union were born two sons, Ruda M. and

William P. Gow, and one daughter, Lillie M, the wife of Rev. H. K. Freeman.

Rev. Gow spent his entire life in the ministry. He was a fearless and tireless preacher of the word. He held pastorates in the states of Michigan, Pennsylvania, Indiana and Ohio, his native state. He has more years of service to his credit than any Baptist preacher in the state of Ohio.

With his passion for souls and seeing the need of laborers he was always encouraging young ministers to preach the word. He has made and baptized thousands of converts. In his earlier life he was very popular in giving patriotic addresses. His last public address was given at the union services held at the Spencerville Federated church, on Good Friday, 1928. During his last illness, even while at the hospital, he would ask people who called to see him if they knew the Lord. He was a good husband and a very affectionate father and a kind and friendly neighbor.

He was survived by wife Cornelia (also a minister), two sons, a daughter, ten grandchildren, and twelve great-grandchildren.

Spouse:
 Cornelia Evangeline White Gow (1860 - 1950)

Children:
 Ruda Marion Gow (1880 - 1969)*
 Lillie Minerva Gow Freeman (1888 - 1973)

Delbert Glendon Gould
Birth:
Sep. 28, 1908
Tom Corwin,
Jackson County,
Ohio
Death:
Jan. 18, 1958
Columbus,
Franklin County,
Ohio
Burial:
Forest Lawn Memorial
Gardens,
Columbus,
Franklin County,
Ohio

He was converted in the Methodist Church at Glenroy, Ohio. Later he became a member of the Wellston Free Will Baptist Church. He went to Columbus where he united with the Free Will Baptist Church on South Parsons Avenue, which later became the Gibbard Free Will Baptist Church. He was called into the ministry and was licensed in 1949 and ordained in 1950. He served the Rosedale Church and then was chosen as the first pastor of Welch Avenue Free Will Baptist Church in February, 1952 which was started by the Gibbard Ave. church. While pastor of this church he had a massive heart attack on the parking lot of the White Cross hospital where he was going to his doctor. He died at death 49 years. This church continues today as the Heritage Free Will Baptist Church as a large church and multiple staff.

Rev Olen L Gould
Birth:
Oct. 9, 1915
Ohio
Death:
Jul. 1, 1989
Ohio
Burial:
Forest Lawn Memorial
Gardens
Columbus
Franklin County
Ohio

He was the son of Grover C. and Pearl H. (Vititoe) GOULD, both b. Ohio. He was married to Grayce E. Widdefield, and they made their home in

Columbus. He worked as a machinist early in their marriage for some time. He became a Free Will Baptist minister at an early age, and was affiliated with the Eastern General Association of Free Will Baptists in the mid-1930. His name appears in the old 1936 Minutes of the Ass'n when it met in Glennville, GA: "Ohio Sunday schools, by Rev. Olen Gould, Wellston, OH, where he had collected offerings for Sun. Schools. Possibly a colleague was Rev. I. B. May, who also attended from Ohio that year. His older brother, Rev. Delbert G GOULD, is also bur. in this cemetery.

James W. Hall
Birth:
May 28, 1909
Death:
Sep. 25, 1941
Burial:
Butler-Martin Cemetery,
Minford, Scioto County, Ohio.

Ira Z. Haning
Birth:
June 1825
Death:
Sep. 27, 1878
Burial:
Calvary Baptist Cemetery,
Rio Grande, Gallia County,
Ohio

Haning was born in Alexander, Ohio.. His parents were first Methodists and later Freewill Baptists, and were faithful in giving religious instruction to their twelve children. Ira was converted in 1843 and joined the church in Lodi, where the family then resided. He studied two years in the University of Ohio at Athens. He also engaged in teaching, and preached at various places acceptably. He received license in February, 1846, and two years later was ordained at Lodi by Rev's Job Kittle, D. C. Tapping, and S. S. Branch. The churches of the

Athens Q. M., then recently formed, needed pastoral care, and he itinerated among them all for several years.. He influenced Deacon Nehemiah Atwood to give $50,000 to start Rio Grande College in southern Ohio which still exist as a popular college.

Death is the crown jewel for the Christian.

Joseph Franklyn Harness
Birth:
Mar. 25, 1916
Greene County, Ohio
Death:
Nov. 20, 1995 Portsmouth, Scioto County, Ohio
Burial:
Lucasville Cemetery, Lucasville, Scioto County, Ohio

He attended Rio Grande College where he played basketball and received his education. His pastorates were mainly in the Porter Conference in southern Ohio. He was a member of the General Board of The Ohio Association Of Free Will Baptist. He also served as the moderator of the state convention on a number of occasions. His voice was readly heard and respected.

Today is not a day of defeat

Henry Lee Hawkins
Birth:
May 24, 191
Kentucky
Death:
May 9, 1993
Wheelersburg, Scioto County, Ohio
Burial:

Memorial Burial Park,
Wheelersburg,
Scioto County, Ohio

Reverend Henry Lee Hawkins was the pastor of several Free Will Baptist churches in southern Ohio, the last of which was Porter Free Will Baptist. He also built many homes and churches in the area and was a skilled craftsman who made many beautiful clocks and pieces of furniture in his later years. He was a strong leader for many years within the Scoio Yearly conference.

Dave A. Hayes
Birth:
Aug. 22, 1889
Lawrence County, Kentucky
Death:
Aug. 28, 1968
Columbus,
Franklin County, Ohio
Burial:
Forest Lawn Memorial
Gardens, Columbus,
Franklin County, Ohio

Retired from Columbus First Freewill Baptist Church in 1964. In the ministry for 50 years. Elected honorary pastor in 1963 Columbus First Freewill Baptist Church.

Hensley Jr., Rev. Richard
1927 – 2020
BIRTH
August 30, 1927
Nolan, W. Va.
DEATH
April 23, 2020
Columbus, Ohio
BURIAL
Franklin Hills Memory Gardens
Mausoleum
Columbus, Ohio

Reverend Richard Hensley Jr. just a sinner saved by grace, age 92, born to the late Richard and Lottie Marcum Hensley.

Reverend Hensley served for 39 years as pastor of South Columbus Freewill Baptist Church.

Reverend Clyde Ferrell and Pastor Tim Stevens officiating.

Herbert J Henson
Birth:
1912
Death:
April 1, 1987
Burial:
Woodlawn Cemetery,
Ada, Hardin County, Ohio

Luther Hecox
Birth:
Dec. 28, 1795
Whitestown,
N. Y.
Death:
Sep. 1, 1878
Meigs County,
Ohio
Burial:
Brick Cemetery,
Meigs County,
Ohio
Hecox was the son of Truman and Sarah Hasford Hecox. His parents settled in Meigs County, Ohio, where he married in 1817 and early became one of the active Free Baptists. After serving as a licentiate several years, he

was ordained in 1850, and continued in the work of the Lord in that vicinity until the infirmities of age compelled him to desist. He was a consistent Christian, pathetic and earnest in preaching. Luther was 81 years old when he died. He was the husband of Matilda Dean and the father of Truman.

Today is not a day of defeat

Abraham Hemmerly
Birth:
Patterson, Jackson Twp.,
Hardin County, Ohio
1846
Death:
King, Washington
1917
Burial:
Jackson Center Cemetery
Kirby, Wyandot County, Ohio

Occupation: Baptist Minister
Event: Graduated 1894
Marion High School, Marion, Ohio

Kendal F. Higgins
Birth:
March 18, 1813
Cayuga County, New York
Death:
May 8, 1887
Union County, Ohio
Burial:
Oakdale Cemetery
Marysville
Union County, Ohio

He was one of the fathers of the Free Baptist ministry in central Ohio. He experienced religion at the age of 12. He moved to Ohio in early life and felt it an imperative duty to enter the ministry. His ordination took place on April 6, 1845, with Elders G. W. Baker, and Arron Hatch and G. H. Moon serving on the Council.

For over 40 years he was an earnest and successful preacher. He had the care of the churches in central and southern Ohio and Indiana. He had an excellent natural ability and was a strong reasoner, and his sermons were clear and strong presentations of gospel truth.

Rev Horace G. Hill
Birth:
1853
Death:
1904
Burial:
Waldren Hill Cemetery
Idaho, Pike County, Ohio

An ordained Free Will Baptist minister from Ohio. Worked in several states.

Jacob Hisey
Birth:
Jul. 30, 1816
Death:
Dec. 26, 1847
Waynesville,
Ohio
Burial:
Miami Cemetery
Corwin
Warren County,
Ohio

He was converted in 1836,

licensed by the Miami Quarterly Meeting in 1843 and spent some time at the Biblical School at Whitestown, New York.

Rev John Hisey
Birth
: Apr. 27, 1821
Death:
Unknown
Burial:
Miami Cemetery
Corwin
Warren County
Ohio

Son of Jacob Hisey, Sr., and Amelia HISEY. Affiliated with the Freewill Bapt. church in Warren Co., and preached in the vicinity. His father, though not a minister, was a faithful, liberal, and exemplary Christian in the FWB church there.

Rev Donald Wayne Hix
Birth:
Feb. 14, 1943
Grove City
Franklin County
Ohio
Death:
Jun. 12, 2017
Urbana
Champaign County
Ohio
Burial:
Jenkins Chapel Cemetery
Urbana
Champaign County
Ohio

Rev. Donald W. Hix, 74, of Woodstock, Ohio went home to be with the Lord in Mercy Memorial Hospital, Urbana. He was born the son of Henry and Edna (Ward) Hix. Rev. Don was ordained in June 1966. In March of 1973, he was called to pastor in his home church, Woodstock Free Will Baptist Church, where he pastored 26 years of his 50 years of pastoral service. He is currently the pastor at the Redeemer Free Will Baptist Church in London (Somerford). He retired from Honda in 2004. Don cherished his wife, adored his children and grandchildren, and led his family by modeling Christ's marriage to the church. There was no better example of how to lead a family than Don Hix. Don enjoyed doing yard work and could often be found mowing the yard, planting flowers, or weeding the garden. Donald was survived by his wife of 56 years, Dorothy Hix; Tamara (Dwayne) Brewer, Tracie (Dale) House and Amy (London)Rogan; grand-children, Dawn, Drake, DeAndra, Destanee, Chelsie, Halie, Tabitha and Jaxon; great grandchildren, Desirae, Dristian, Jocelyn, Zayden, Kailynn and Kane, sister, Linda (Rev. Jim) Blankenship as well as several nieces and nephews. He was preceded in death by his parents, siblings, Russell "Bud", Carl, Robert and Mildred.

Woodstock Free Will Baptist Church, 332 W. Bennett St., Woodstock, Ohio. A

Celebration of Life service was held at the church with Pastor Mike Mounts officiating.

William Hooper
Birth:
Dec. 2, 1818
Death:
Mar. 21, 1877
Burial:
Miles Cemetery
Rutland, Meigs County, Ohio

Rev. William Hooper, M. D. was a native of New Jersey, was converted at Alexander, Ohio, where he was soon licensed to preach, and ordained a few years later. He labored as an itinerant minister in Athens, Meigs, Gallia, Lawrence and Scioto Counties twelve years, and gathered one or two churches. He then turned his attention to medicine, graduating from the Starling Medical College at Columbus in 1857, and devoted but little time to ministerial duties. He died at age 58 years.

Rev Sardine P. Humphrey
Birth:
Feb. 2, 1862
Rutland
Meigs County
Ohio
Death:
1934
Ohio
Burial:
Woodlawn Cemetery
Toledo
Lucas County
Ohio

Elder Jonathan Hoyt
Birth:
Apr. 19, 1772
Litchfield
Litchfield County,Connecticut
Death:
Apr. 12, 1840
Scioto County,Ohio
Burial:
Turner Cemetery
Scioto County,Ohio

Spouse: Peggy Taylor Hoyt, Marriage: Abt 1794 - Litchfield, Connecticut, United States.

Rev. Sardine P. Humphrey, son of William G. and Sarah B. (Cook) He was educated at Rio Grande College, and was principal of the Middleport High School. In 1884, he received license to preach, and Jan. 1, 1886, he was ordained by Rev. W. J. Fulton, and others. For a time had charge of the church at Camaam.(OH).

Cyrus Cordon Inman
Birth:
Jan 21, 1839
Spencer, Ohio
Death:
1917
Burial:
Spencer Cemetery,
Spencer
Medina County,
Ohio

A worthy and esteemed minister of the Freewill Baptist church in Randall's movement. He attended Hillsdale FWB College in Hillsdale, MI, and organized and pastored churches. He was married to Clemma C. Smith. He was the son of Deacon Stephen Inman, b.

1808 NY, and prob. charter members of that Spencer church. He was for a few years pastor of churches in the Oceana Q. M., Mich. He was ordained in 1869, and not long after returned to Ohio and took charge of the Spencer church, and was pastor of the Beebetown church in the Cleveland Q. M. Cyrus also served in the Civil War from Ohio, Ohio 124th Inf. Regiment, Co. B, as Cpl, then promoted to Sgt. Mustered out 1865.

John Jeffrey
Birth:
Unknown
Death:
Ohio
Burial:
Resthaven Memory Gardens
Avon
Lorain County,

Ohio

He was an early Free Will Baptist minister in northern Ohio that began the Vincent FWB church. He was a missionary, pastor and known servant.

Even Death Is Not To Be Feared By One Who Has Lived Wisely.

John Robert Kemper
Birth:
1875
Death:
1957
Scioto County, Ohio
Burial:
Vernon Cemetery,
Lyra, Scioto County, Ohio,

Early pastor in Southern Ohio. Pastor of Union Free Will Baptist church for many years.

Marcus Kilbourn
Birth:
1790
Vermont
Death:
Nov. 28, 1836
Delaware County
Ohio
Burial:
Wyatt Cemetery
Waldo
Marion County, Ohio

Rev. Marcus Kilborn a native of Connecticut, experienced religion in Alexandria, NY, in 1816, and ordained in Ohio in 1820.

That same year he organized the First Free Baptist church in Indiana, the Bryant's Creek (later Randall) church. He also labored in southwestern Ohio, making his home at Maineville. He assisted in organizing the Miami Quarterly Meeting, and the Ohio Yearly Meeting. He was a faithful pioneer minister, and died triumphantly in 1837.

Ohio marriage records show he married Mary Price, 11 June 1818, Scioto, OH, by Rev. Rufus Cheney. [a companion in the ministry].

It was said of him that he was a pious man, and built up churches. He often traveled on foot, leaving wife and babies at home, and not having much of the world's goods. His wife passed on before he did.

Inscription:
Aged 41 Years

Howard Kimble
Birth:
Unknown
Death:
Unknown
Lawrence County, Ohio
Burial:
Oakland Chapel Cemetery,
Kitts Hill,
Lawrence County, Ohio

A well-known minister in southern Ohio and northeast Kentucky remembered for pastoring Brush Creek in Ky.

and the Union Church near Wheelersburg, Ohio. He was a member of the Ohio Board of Directors.

Jobe Kittle
Birth:
Apr. 28, 1805
Death:
Mar. 26, 1877
Scioto County, Ohio
Burial:
Old Wheelersburg Cemetery
Wheelersburg
Scioto County, Ohio

He had been a member of the Porter church 44 years. Receiving ordination to the ministry in 1841, at the hands of Rev. J. M. Shurtliff and others. He labored faithfully for the cause of Christ in the Little Scioto Quarterly Meeting.

Clayton Dale Lawhorn
BIRTH
23 Apr 1935
Olive Hill, KY,
DEATH
25 Jun 2019 (aged 84)
BURIAL
Mansfield Cemetery
Mansfield,
Richland County, Ohio,

Clayton was born to Perry J. and Margaret (Bare) Lawhorn. He proudly served his country in the U.S. Army, during the Korean War. He was a member of Dean Road Freewill Baptist Church. Clayton enjoyed fishing, hunting, traveling with family, and singing. He held many revivals in his travels. He was devoted to his family .Full Military Honors performed by the R.C. Joint Veterans Burial Detail.

George W Lawrence
Birth:
Jun. 2, 1854
Dover
Kent, England
Death:
Jul. 26, 1932
Geneva
Ashtabula County
Ohio
Burial:
Cherry Valley Cemetery
Cherry Valley
Ashtabula County, Ohio

He was brought to America by his parents when a year old, and lived on a farm till nine, had the benefit of the district school three months in the year. He came to Hillsdale in 1874 and took the A. B. degree in 1880. He spend the next year in special study at Normal, Illinois. He was rhen the Principal of the Academy at Pierpoint, Ohio, for two years, but moved to Kansas in 1883. In the following spring he became Principal of the High school at Jellico, Tennessee, and held the position until May 18, 1888, when he was shot down by a drunken hireling for his temperance principles. The next nine years were spent in Illinois, Michigan, and Iowa seeking to recover his shattered health, but in 1897, by solicitation of Rev. and Mrs. A.A. Myers, he went to Cumberland Gap, Tennessee, where he was an Instructor in Mathematic in Lincoln Memorial University. While at Hillsdale he was identified with the Theological Society, and his loyalty and that of his brother were the founders of the Lawrence Prize beginning in the spring of 1879. George Lawrence was the brother of Richard M. Lawrence, and Alfred Hogbin and they were children of John & Mary Hogbin. George & Richard changed their last name when they attended college in Hillsdale, Michigan. Death

Age: 78 years 1 month 24 days. Spouse's Name: Angelia A. Lawrence.

Claudis Lewis
Birth: Jul. 8, 1922
Johnson County, Kentucky
Death:
Sep. 28, 2003
Franklin. Ohio
Burial:
Springboro Cemetery,
Springboro,
Warren County, Ohio

Lewis was a World War II veteran of the United States Army and was an escort to Gen. George S. Patton and General Dwight D. Eisenhower. He was a member of the Franklin Free Will Baptist Church. His funeral was held at the Franklin Church with the Rev. Dencil Owsley officiating with full military honors.

James Littlejohn
Birth:
Sep. 8, 1820
Ohio
Death:
Nov. 27, 1884
Wheelersburg, Scioto County
Ohio
Burial:
Old Wheelersburg Cemetery
Wheelersburg
Scioto County, Ohio

James Littlejohn was the son of John & Lucy Littlejohn and the husband of Cynthia Smith md October 12, 1843 Scioto Co., Oh. They were the parents of three children.
His name appears in the FWB Register 1858 as a minister from the Green FWB church.

Rev Edgar N Long
Birth:
1885
Death:
1959
Burial:
City View Cemetery
Salem
Marion County
Oregon, USA
Plot: Sec. U

He was on the 37th session program in 1907at the west Mansfield FWB Church. He preached on Wednesday and address on the Subject, What Free-will Baptist stand for after George Barnard had spoken on What Regular Baptist Stand for. E. N. Long addressed, Is union of Free-will Baptists with regular Baptist Desirable?

Charles Lykins
Birth:
Aug. 7, 1907
Death:
Mar. 5, 1978
Ohio
Burial:
South Webster Cemetery,

South Webster,
Scioto County,
Ohio

Minister in southern Ohio.

Bobby J Lyons
Birth:
Mar. 13, 1940
Death:
Oct. 13, 2007
Burial:
Plattsburg Cemetery,
Plattsburg, Clark County,
Ohio

He was a member of the Eastside Free Will Baptist church and a Korean veteran.

David Marks
Birth:
Nov. 14, 1805
Shandaken,
Ulster
County, New York
Death:
Dec. 15, 1845

Oberlin, Lorain County, Ohio
Burial::
Westwood Cemetery,
Oberlin, Lorain County, Ohio,
Plot: Sect. F, Lot 5

Rev. Marks, as a child, felt impressed that God was calling him to a great work and began preaching at age 15 years. He traveled all over New England preaching to large crowds wanting to hear "the boy preacher." At 13 yrs of age, he walked over 368 miles from his home in New York to Providence, Rhode Island to attend Brown University where he had free tuition, but no further assistance towards room and board could be rendered; with sad heart, he walked back home. He had a thirst for knowledge and immediately began to study and read while walking or riding horse-back to another preaching appointment in his itinerant ministry. He found he was in sentiment with the teaching of 'Free Will, free grace and free salvation' and united with the Free Will Baptists in July 1819. He became a leader in that church and in the 1831 General Conference, was appointed Agent of the newly established Book Concern, a publishing house, which position he held for four years, leading it to solid footing financially.

He also was an ardent promoter of Home and Foreign Missions and Education societies. He held pastorates in New Hampshire, Rhode Island, New York, and organized a church in Rochester, New York, and had an iterant ministry all over New England, Upper Canada, and into Ohio. He kept a journal and a "Narrative" of his work and ministry which was printed in 1831, at the insistence of others. After his death, his wife,

DAVID MARKS.

Marilla, edited *"Memoirs of David Marks"* which was published by the FWB Printing Establishment in 1846; William Burr, Printer. He went to Oberlin College in

Ohio, a place of abolitionist creativity and thought, he having carried the same sentiments in his church and life. He had spoken, written and labored to see slavery abolished. He was without a doubt, one of the most esteemed ministers of his day in his church and in the public's eye. It was while in Oberlin with his wife, that his health failed even more. His great desire to preach even in his weakened condition was so great that he requested that "I be carried to the meeting house to give one more talk for God before I die." This they did, even though it was thought he would die before he finished, but he lived a few weeks longer. Dr. Charles G. Finney of Oberlin preached his funeral. Finney said of Mark's "There is none greater among Free Will Baptists."

His wife published his memoirs entitled, "The Life of David Marks."

His sister Elizabeth was the first woman to graduate from Oberlin as a lady minister. He had a brother and nephew who went on to Kansas and began the FWB work there. They are listed under the Kansas section herein.

Herman Marcum
Birth:
Apr. 3, 1933
Wayne County,
West Virginia
Death:
Feb. 7, 2012
Orlando, FL
Burial:
Union Cemetery,
Columbus,
Franklin County, Ohio

He was pastor of the Philadelphia Free Will Baptist Church before his retirement to Florida. For 20 years he raised money locally by coordinating walk-a-thons and rock-a-thons, used for donating fruit baskets to nursing homes in the Columbus area. Rev. Marcum was a member of Faith Freewill Baptist Church in Orlando, FL.

Marvin Dale Markin
Birth:
Aug. 14, 1937
Vinton County,
Ohio
Death:
Jun. 3, 2010
Athens, Athens County, Ohio
Burial:
Harkins Chapel Cemetery,
Bolins Mills,
Vinton County,
Ohio

Free Will Baptist pastor is southeast Ohio and active in his district and state associations. He had been a minister for 53 years with 22 years at Black Oak FWB.

Amos P. Marmon
Birth:
Unknown
Death:
Nov. 28, 1879
Burial:
Marmon Valley Cemetery
East Liberty,
Logan County, Ohio

Amos Marmon's parents were Edmund Marmon, 1786-1831, and Sarah (Stanton) Marmon, 1788--.He married Cynthia Ann Outland, (1830-1903). Amos P. Marmon, was born in Marmon Valley, Ohio and died near his native place. He was converted under the ministry of Rev. O.E. Baker and united with the East Liberty church in 1853. He proved himself a useful member, and was ordained June 3, 1872. His sermons were thoughtful and carefully prepared, and being deeply emotional, his words touched many hearts.
He was age 53 years, 3 months and 14 days at his death.

James W Martin
Birth:
Jul. 11, 1829
Guernsey County, Ohio
Death:
Oct. 28, 1899
Athens County, Ohio
Burial:
Crossroads Cemetery
Albany, Athens County, Ohio

Rev. James W. Martin, was the son of James H. and Tracy (Triplett) MARTIN, and was married to Jane Gibson, April 15, 1852. To them were born three children. He was educated at the Albany Academy and the Ohio University; was converted in 1860 and ordained May 23, 1868. He has held the pastorates of several churches in the Ohio River Yearly Meeting to which his ministry has been spent conducting revivals, baptizing a large number of converts and organizing one church. He has been influential in the local denominational gatherings, and has served as trustee of Rio Grande College and of the Ohio State Association, as president of the board of Atwood Institute, and several times as a delegate to the General Conference.

Eugene Martin
Birth:
1910
Death:
Unknown
Scioto County, Ohio
Burial:
Bennett Cemetery,
Minford, Scioto County, Ohio

Moses Walter Martin
Birth:
Apr. 10, 1887
Scioto County, Ohio

Death:
Dec. 18, 1964
Portsmouth,
Scioto County, Ohio
Burial:
Old Wheelersburg Cemetery
Scioto County, Ohio

Moses and his family moved to Portsmouth where he was employed as a street car conductor on the Portsmouth to Sciotoville run. In 1921 the family moved back to Dogwood Ridge in Wheelersburg where he farmed. Later he moved and was employed as a locomotive fireman and engineer at the local Wheeling Steel plant in New Boston. He worked for the steel mill until he retired at the age of 70 (1957). Moses was an ordained Free Will Baptist minister and served several churches in the Scioto County area.

Chester A. Masters
Birth:
Dec. 9, 1928
Lewis Couny, Kentucky
Death:
Jun. 12, 2012
Mansfield, Richland County, Ohio
Burial:
Franklin Cemetery, Mansfield, Richland County, Ohio

He was a bi-vocational Free Will Baptist minister who retired from the Empire Detroit Steel. He was a veteran of the United States Army. At the cemetery he was given full military honors by the Richland County Joint Veterans Burial Detail.

Virgil Ouinton Masters
Birth:
Oct. 10, 1926
Lewis County
Kentucky
Death:
Dec. 23, 2014
Burial:

Springmill Cemetery
Mansfield
Richland County, Ohio

Virgil Q. Masters, 88, was the son of Ora and Celia (Zornes) Masters. A faithful, pleasant, generous man, Virgil served as a Corporal in the Army from 1942 until 1952, serving in Korea and Japan. He retired from Stone Container where he was a Teamster Local #40 truck driver. A member of Dean Road Freewill Baptist Church, Virgil served as assistant Pastor for 8 years and Pastor for 32 years.

Funeral services was conducted by Rev. Clifford Earl Tackett and Pastor Randy Nichols. Military services conducted by the Richland County Joint Veterans Burial Detail.

Irey Berdell May
Birth:
Mar. 24, 1899
Pennsylvania
Death:

Dec. 15, 1970
Brecksville
Cuyahoga County
Ohio
Burial:
Grandview Cemetery
Salem
Columbiana County, Ohio

He was also a minister and represented Ohio Yearly Meeting in the 1936 Eastern General Association of Free Will Baptists, when in session in Glennville, GA. Per 1940 census had a wife Annabel age 24 and a son Robert L age 2 in house - living in Salem Ohio.

Isaac May
Birth:
Oct. 5, 1796
Strafford,
Orange County,
Vermont
Death:
Dec. 8, 1874
Clyde

Sandusky County, Ohio
Burial:
Ellsworth Cemetery
Clyde
Sandusky County, Ohio

He was the son of Harvey May Joanne (Wedge); husband of (1) Racheal McMillen, (2) Nancy McMillen. approx 16 children between the two marriages. He was converted at age 18 and united with the Christian denomination. Later he joined the York church in Ohio and was ordained by the Huron Quarterly Meeting in 1831. For some time he labored as an itinerant: after which he settled at Townsend, and organized a church and remained with it the remainder of his life.

Rev Lovell J May
Birth:
May 2, 1929
Death:
Nov. 27, 2017
Burial:
Obetz Cemetery
Obetz
Franklin County,
Ohio

Reverend Lovell J. May, age 88, Retired pastor with Canaan Land Free Will Baptist Church. Pastored for

several CCU and Hilltop Community Church. Member of UAW Local 969. U.S. Army Veteran. Served in Army and Navy Reserve and National Guard.
Preceded in death by twin brother, Lowell, brother, George Jr., sisters, Vivian Eicher, Joyce Holbrook, Elsie Saxour.
Survived by wife of 71 years, Wanda May; children, Steven May, Sharon (Michael) Adams, and Ronald (Cindy) May; grandchildren, Todd, Tami, Tara, Jennifer, Joseph, Justin, Jim, Makenna, Elana, and Ethan; 14 great-grandchildren; 3 great-great-grandchildren; many nieces, nephews, other relatives and friends.

Arthur "Pete" Maynard
Birth:
Jul. 14, 1939
Beauty,
Martin County, Kentucky
Feb. 21, 2002
Washington Court House
Fayette County,
Ohio
Burial:
New Holland Cemetery,
New Holland,
Pickaway County, Ohio

He was founder of the Woodlawn Free Will Baptist

Church in Washington Courthouse. He served his country in the United States Navy during the Vietnam era, and as a bi-vocational minister. He was employed as a corrections officer with Ohio Dept. of Corrections in Pickaway County.

Rev Robert Lee Maynard
Birth:
Mar. 10, 1938
Beauty
Martin County,
Kentucky
Death:
Aug. 12, 2014
Columbus
Franklin County,
Ohio
Burial:
New Holland Cemetery
New Holland
Pickaway County,
Ohio

Bob was a Free Will Baptist Minister and a member of the Capital City Conference of Free Will Baptists and faithful member and minister of the Heritage Free Will Baptist Church of Columbus, OH.

Billy O. McCarty
Birth:
Aug. 7, 1926
Salyersville,
Magoffin County,
Kentucky
Death:
Jan. 8, 2008
Springfield,
Clark County,
Ohio
Burial:
South Vienna Cemetery,
South Vienna,
Clark County,
Ohio

He ministered in Free Will Baptist churches in Urbana, West Jefferson, Youngstown, Ohio; California and Georgia during his long ministry. He was actively involved with the Family Life Ministries of Tennessee. He was a man of patient compassion and a wise counselor.

Rev Sturgell McCarty
Birth:
Jan. 29, 1923
Magoffin County
Kentucky
Death:
Apr. 19, 2016
Springfield
Clark County
,Ohio
Burial:
Maple Grove Cemetery
Mechanicsburg
Champaign County,
Ohio

Age-93 at the time of his passing.

Besides his parents, he was preceded in death by his wife and mother of his 2 daughters, Recie Deloris (Miller) McCarty, brothers: Chatham, Herchell, Willard, Reverend Billy O. and Reverend Cecil McCarty.

He served 1 year in the 3c's, and the US Army during WW 11, in the European Theater. Became an ordained Freewill Baptist Minister in 1953, serving several churches in the Clark, Champaign, and Franklin Counties along with several other denominations in the area.

William McCarty
Birth:
Sep. 16, 1938
Death:
Feb. 2, 1984
Lawrence County, Ohio
Burial:
Aid Cemetery,
Aid, Lawrence County, Ohio

He pastored the Fox Hollow and Symes Valley FWB churches in Lawrence Co., Ohio.

Alva McDaniel, Sr
Birth:
1907
Death:
Unknown
Scioto County,
Ohio
Burial:
White Gravel Cemetery,
Minford,
Scioto County, Ohio

Robert Lee Meade
Birth: Jul. 11, 1930
Portsmouth,
Scioto County, Ohio
Death:
Mar. 23, 2001
Springfield,
Clark County, Ohio
Burial:
Ferncliff Cemetery,
Springfield,
Clark County, Ohio

He was ordained as minister in 1954 and was State Evangelist for four years. He served as pastor in six different churches from 1956 to 1993: The Shumway Freewill Baptist Church, Houston Hollow Freewill Baptist Church, The Fairborn Church, Turkey Creek Freewill Baptist Church, Belmont Freewill Baptist Church, and twenty-two years at the Forest Valley Freewill Baptist Church, where he was a member.

Redford Meadows
Birth:
Feb. 12, 1925
Wittensville, Ky
Death:
Apr. 6, 2007
Ironton, Ohio
Burial:
Rose Hill Burial Park and Mausoleum, Ashland, Boyd County, Kentucky, Plot:F

Meadows was a Free Will Baptist Minister for more than 50 years and pastored churches in Michigan, Ohio and Kentucky.
His more recent ministry was at the Union Free Will Baptist Church near Wheelersburg, Ohio

Russell Milam
Birth: 1882
Death:
1967
Scioto County, Ohio
Burial:
Bennett Cemetery,
Minford,
Scioto County, Ohio

Early leader in the district, state, and national programs of the Free Will Baptists. His name appears on a regular basis as a representive from Ohio on the national General Board. He was the publicity chairman when the nation convention met in Huntington, WVA.

Bert Miller
Birth:
Feb.21, 1913
Death:
Apr. 5, 2001
Burial:
Obetz Cemetery,
Obetz,
Franklin County, Ohio

Ordained a Minister in 1935 and instrumental in starting many Freewill Baptist Churches. In 1968 he founded and pastored Lockbourne Freewill Baptist Church in Lockbourne, Ohio. In 1992 Rev. Miller oversaw the building of the new church on Rohr Rd. where he continued to pastor until his death. Past President for 16 years of TWU Local #208. Retired from COTA after 35 years..

Troy Miller
Birth:
Sep. 11, 1942
Wonder, Floyd County,
Kentucky
Death:
Aug. 18, 2012
Jackson, Jackson County,
Ohio
Burial:
Franklin Valley Cemetery,
Wellston, Jackson County,
Ohio

Troy Miller was born in the hills of eastern Kentucky 30 minutes from the Prestonsburg area. His family moved to West Virginia and Clyde, Ohio before settling in Jackson, Ohio. It was here that he met and married his high school sweetheart, Janice Forshey, in 1958. Together they had 3 sons and 1 daughter: Bob, Julie, Brian, and Jamie. At the approximate age of 25, Troy accepted Christ as his Savior and soon felt the call to go into the ministry. He would go on to pastor the Coalton

Free Will Baptist church on three separate occasions, the Glenroy FWB church (both in Jackson county), and would re-open the Bethesda Chapel FWB church in Pike county after it had closed its doors several years earlier. During this time he held many revivals, performed hundreds of weddings and funerals and became well known throughout the community. He continued in the ministry until April of 2012 by serving as clergy member for Four Winds Nursing Home in Jackson. In 1995, Troy was diagnosed with kidney cancer and underwent surgery to completely remove one kidney and a portion of the other. He remained cancer free until 2008, when he was diagnosed once again with kidney cancer, this time terminal. Troy Miller passed away in Kingston, Ohio in Ross County at the home of his youngest son.

Troy was formerly employed at Pillsbury in Wellston. He enjoyed visiting and ministering to the residents at Heartland and Four Winds Nursing Homes, as well as ministering to others through his weekly radio broadcasts.

Gerald G. Moore
Birth:
Mar. 9, 1931
Clintwood, Dickenson County,
Virginia
Death:
Jul. 9, 2009
Sandusky County, Ohio,
Burial:
McPherson Cemetery,
Clyde,
Sandusky County, Ohio,

Member of the First Freewill Baptist Church in Clyde, Ohio. He served his country in the Air Force during the Korean War. Mr. Moore was a bi-vocational minister had also worked 34 years at the Whirlpool Corp in Clyde.

Rev Milo Moore
Birth:
Jan. 8, 1887
Carterville
Williamson County
Illinois
Death:
Mar. 30, 1974
Gallipolis
Gallia County, Ohio
Burial:
Mound Hill Cemetery
Gallipolis
Gallia County
Ohio
He pastored the Bryan First FWB church in Texas in 1926.

Richmond Center
Ashtabula County, Ohio

Tommy Moore
Birth:
Sep. 19, 1928
Adams, Lawrence County,
Kentucky
Death:
Sep. 23, 1967
Burial:
Yatesville Cemetery, Louisa,
Lawrence County, Kentucky

He was the third pastor of the Welch Avenue Free Will Baptist Church in Columbus, Ohio.

Horace Morse
Birth:
Sep. 19, 1795
Worthington
Hampshire County,
Massachusetts
Death:
Nov. 24, 1854
Williamsfield
Ashtabula County, Ohio
Burial:
Richmond Center Cemetery

He moved to northern Ohio in 1810 where for several years he was engaged in teaching school. In 1818 he married Lydia, a daughter of Judge S. Stanton. He was converted in the revival which led to the formation of the Williamsfield church, of which he was one of the original members, and he immediately began preaching. He was active in the formation of the Wayne Quarterly Meeting and for some years was a leading minister in the Crawford and Ashtabula Quarterly Meetings.

Inscription:
Rev. HORACE MORSE
WHO DIED Nov. 24, 1854
60 yrs. 2 mos. 6 days (rest of script not legible from photo)

Kevin Willard Morris

Birth:
Sep. 13, 1978
Mansfield, Richland County, Ohio
Death:
Nov. 21, 2008
Plymouth, Richland County, Ohio
Burial:
Greenlawn Cemetery, Plymouth, Richland County, Ohio

He preached the Gospel for 12 years, serving as pastor at Paradise Free Will Baptist Church two years. He graduated from Pioneer Career and Technical Center where he received the Byron Carmean Award-an award granted to non-traditional students and received his Associate's Degree in Early Childhood Education at The Ohio State University. At the age of 11, he underwent a heart transplant, a very special gift allowing him to spend 19 more years with his family and friends.

William Moses

Birth:
Unknown
Death:
Oct. 26, 1879
Cincinnati, Ohio
Burial:
Spring Grove Cemetery Cincinnati, Hamilton County, Ohio
Plot: Garden LN, Section 14, Lot 0, Space 262

Moses was a native of Connecticut and one of the early New York ministers, having been ordained in 1814. In 1832 he was connected with the Betheny Q. M., and after that time, until 1857, with the churches of the Genesee Q. M. Here he preached and labored faithfully. After this he spent about twenty years in Ripon, Wis., and, a year before his death, went to live with his children in Cincinnati. His wife, with whom he had lived sixty-two years

Albanus Avery Moulton

Birth:
Mar. 23, 1848
Massachusetts
Death:
Jun. 22, 1888
Colorado
Burial:
Calvary Baptist Cemetery,
Rio Grande,
Gallia County,Ohio

He took the freshman year of his college course at Bates College, the sophomore year at Hillsdale College, and the junior and senior years at Yale College, where he took honors and graduated in 1871. He then completed a course in mathematics and civil engineering in the University of Michigan, and worked for a time at railroad surveying. He was made professor of mathematics at Rio Grande College at its opening in 1876. Three years later he was made president. He discharged the duties of this position for six years with the highest degree of ability, zeal and success. In 1887, it was manifest he could not serve the college longer. His last three years were spent in Colorado, where he worked some at teaching and surveying. His noble Christian spirit made its impression on his schoolmates even, and was

felt still more by the young people under his care at Rio Grande. In this influence to shape its opening years, the college was greatly favored.

Albanus K Moulton

Birth:
Sep. 26, 1810
Hatley, Quebec, Canada
Death:
Jun. 19, 1873
Linndale,
Cuyahoga County, Ohio
Burial:
Woodland Cemetery,
Cleveland,
Cuyahoga County, Ohio,
Plot: Section 40 Lot 84

Like others of the family he was early converted to Christ, and an accident, partially disqualifying him for manual labor, was the occasion of more schooling than was usually enjoyed by boys in his circumstances. While hesitating to devote himself to the ministry, he providentially found himself in 1837 at Mecca, Ohio, at the August session of the Ashtabula Quarterly Meeting, at which Ransom Dunn was ordained. Brother Moulton's position was understood; and the ordination services, with special prayer for him and special exhortation and persuasion by Rev's Wire, Miller and Dunn, resulted in suspending his journey to the South. A congregation was formed from which other preachers were intentionally detained, and thus he was almost compelled to preach his first sermon. From this time he labored faithfully. In October he received license and the next August was ordained by the Geauga Quarterly Meeting at Burton.. Many souls were converted and two or three churches organized. under Brother Moulton's labors in the Geauga Quarterly Meeting the next few years. In 1841 he settled with the Washington Street church, Dover, N. H., where an extensive revival was enjoyed, and a house of worship commenced which was completed the year after he left. Early in 1843 he commenced a successful pastorate in Portland, Me., the church being greatly strengthened. The church in Roxbury, Mass., secured his services in 1848, and the outlook became more encouraging than in any previous field but the church in Lowell was in great need and he soon began with them a useful pastorate, during which they erected a house of worship. But in these years of earnest labor his nervous system became debilitated and he retired to the prairies of Iowa, where with returning health he preached some and edited a weekly paper. In 1860 he returned to active work and labored effectually at Great Falls, New Hampshire., Auburn, Maine, Concord, New Hampshire, and Cleveland, Ohio. His death was instantaneous, resulting from a fall from a bridge at Linndale, a suburb of Cleveland.

Rev Carl Muncy
Birth:
Oct. 27, 1953
Wayne County, West Virginia
Death:
Mar. 2, 2016
Jackson
Jackson County, Ohio
Burial:
Salem Cemetery
Jackson County Ohio

Carl was a loving father, grandpa, and preacher. He loved his family and they will miss him dearly. He was a preacher, Sunday school teacher, and he had a monthly appointment at Edgewood Manor where he sang and read scriptures to the residents. Burial with Pastor Burley Muncy officiating.

Curtis Muncy
Birth:
1943
Death:
July 4, 2018

Burial:
Obetz Cemetery
Obetz, Ohio

Brother Curtis Muncy, 75 years old went home to be with the Lord. He was a true, honest and hardworking man all his life. He left his mark on each and every person he met and he will be missed by many. Services was at the Greater Vision Free Will Baptist Church, Groveport, OH where he served as pastor for many years. The Funeral Service will be held by Pastors Ken Allen and Bob Perry officiating.

James R Music, Sr
Birth:
Dec. 22, 1926
Meally,
Johnson County, Kentucky
Death:
Nov. 10, 2008
Ohio
Burial:
Kingwood Memorial Park,
Lewis Center,
Delaware County, Ohio,

He ministered in several Free Will Baptist churches including Columbus First FWB and Lockbourne FWB.

Homer Nelson

Birth:
1912
Sciotodale,
Scioto County
Ohio
Death:
Apr. 27, 1985,
Portsmouth
Scioto County, Ohio
Burial:
South Webster Cemetery,
South Webster,
Scioto County, Ohio

He was a active Free Will Baptist pastor and denominational leader. He retired after 50 years' service and was a member of the Union Free Will Baptist Church. He was the former pastor of the Germany Hollow, Garden City, Sciotodale, Powellsville, Tick Ridge and the Union churches. He also had been the State Evangelist for the Ohio Free Will Baptist Convention and was the clerk for the Ohio State Association for a number of years. He served as the editor of the *Ambassador Magazine* from 1962 to 1972. His abilities and activities in the denomination are well recorded.

William "Junior" Naves, Jr

Birth:
Apr. 23, 1926
Limestone County, Alabama
Death:
Jul. 22, 2013
Holland
Lucas County, Ohio
Burial:
Ottawa Hills Memorial Park
Ottawa Hills
Lucas County, Ohio

William "Junior" Naves, Jr. was the son of William and

Sarah (Scroggins) Naves, Sr. He married in Athens, Alabama on December 11, 1948. A WWII Navy Veteran, Junior was the Pastor of the Liberty Free Will Baptist Church for over 30 years, as well as a freight handler for Interstate Motor Freight for over 22 years.

Clarence J. Newman
Birth:
Sep. 30, 1925
Huntington, Cabell County,
West Virginia
Death:
May 18, 2002
Ohio
Burial:
Forest Grove Cemetery.
Plain City.
Madison County.
Ohio

Rev. Newman was converted at the age of 12, called to preach in 1957, ordained to the ministry in 1958. His ministry spread over 45 years, with most of it spent in the state of Ohio and with 10 years in Arizona. He was best remembered for his pastorates at the West Jefferson and Marysville Free Will Baptist Churches in Ohio. He served as moderator of the Ohio State Association and as its Promotional Sec. He was a powerful preacher with a distinctive voice conducting revivals in 16 states. He noted his best revival was at the FWB Church in Cleveland in the 1960s, where 75 were saved in one week. During World War II he served in the Merchant Marines. He was a classic car collector and was the 1969 Grand National winner with his 1969 Mustang convertible. He was known for taking small churches and building them into a renewable health.

Rev George S Oiler

Birth:
Mar. 11, 1902
Ewington
Gallia County, Ohio
Death:
Mar. 26, 1983
Pomeroy
Meigs County, Ohio
Burial:
Gravel Hill Cemetery
Cheshire
Gallia County, Ohio

The Rev. George S. Oiler, 81, Racine, died at Veterans Memorial Hospital.

He was born son of the late Andrew J. and Mary Hutchinson Oiler. He was also preceded in death by his first wife, Georgie Frazier Oiler, three brothers and a sister.

At the time of his death, the Mr. Oiler was the minister of the Syracuse Church of God. He had been a minister for 59 years serving several churches over that period. He also had been the owner and operator of coal mines in both Meigs and Gallia Counties for 30 years. He was a member of the West Virginia and Ohio Ministerial Associations.

Surviving are his wife, Virginia L. Gibbs Oiler, Racine; a daughter, Mrs. Ithamer (Mona Lee) Neal, Middleport; a son, Gene Oiler, Middleport; two granddaughters, Janet Russell, Pomeroy, and Lisa Oiler, Middleport; a grandson, Eric Oiler, Middleport; a great-grandson, Ryan Russell, Pomeroy; a stepdaughter, Karen Lyons, Racine; two stepsons, Mike Nease, Pomeroy, and Mitch Nease, Racine; four step-granddaughters, Melanie and Amber Lyons, Racine, and Cassie and Jennifer Nease, Pomeroy; two sisters, Clara Short, Florida, and Lenora Jenkins, Syracuse; a brother, Marion Oiler, Little Hocking, and several nieces and nephews. *Pomeroy Times-Sentinel* March 27, 1983. (Bio by: Robert V Darst)

Inscription:
OILER
MINISTER
FATHER
GEORGE S.
1902 - 1983

Rev Harold Owens

Birth:
Mar. 25, 1944
Carter Co., Kentucky
Death:
Nov. 18, 2016
Mansfield, Ohio
Burial:
Mount Hope Cemetery
Shiloh
Richland County, Ohio

Harold was born to Art and Tina (Stone) Owens. Harold enjoyed preaching and was a member of Dean Road Freewill Baptist Church. He enjoyed playing guitar and singing and spending time outside with his family and friends. He worked at Voisard for 35 years where he retired. Funeral Services with Brother Earl Tackett officiating.

Isaac Tirrell Packard
Birth:
May 3, 1826
Cummington
Hampshire County,
Massachusetts
Death:
May 21, 1849
Licking County, Ohio
Burial:
Old Fredonia Cemetery
Licking County,

Ohio

Isaac was the son of Theophillus and Esther Packard, born in Mass. When about seven years his father removed to Ohio, where he became an honored resident. His mother died when he was eight yrs of age, missing his best friend and counsellor. He went, after this, to live with a responsible family in Licking Co., where he remained several years. He came under the preaching of Rev. Geo. W. Baker, and at about sixteen years of age he began attending the Granville Academy. Afterward, he entered upon the business of teaching. In 1844, he spent about nine months in KY in this employment, when he was prevented by an attack of fever, implicating his lungs. After a few weeks recuperating, he returned to Ohio to his family and friends. He united with the Freewill Baptists at Liberty, was baptized by Rev. Goodwin Evans, a FWB minister. He soon felt impressed to enter the work of the Christian ministry. He received license by the First FWB church in Liberty, Licking Co., April 11, 1846. He received public ordination in May 28, 1848. He rode horseback through the western counties of the State, preaching from place to place, then spent the winter teaching and filling in regular preaching appointments. Again, he entered a course of study in Granville College in early 1848, but constant preaching and studies began to prey upon his feeble bodily powers and his health became much impaired. His disease was such that he knew his time was short. He made disposition of his books to his family, chose President Bailey, of Granville College to preach his funeral. He requested that he be buried beside his mother and sister-- and on May 21, 1849, with his devoted sister and a minister by his bedside, he passed peacefully to the other world. It is written, that "those who knew him best, esteemed him most. He was a young man of uncommon promise. He was mild, modest, and affable in all the intercourse of life, and was greatly endeared to many hearts."

Seth Parker
Birth:
Jul. 7, 1802
New York
Death:
Oct. 19, 1868
New York
Burial:

Steuben Cemetery
Steuben, Huron County, Ohio
Parker was a native of New York and moved to Ohio in 1820. He was converted in 1828, ordained in 1839, and continued with the churches of the Huron Q. M. until his death in Greenfield, Ohio Oct. 19, 1868, aged 66 years. He was twice a delegate to the General Conference, was corporator of the Printing Establishment from 1835 to 1847, and associate judge of the Court of Common Pleas from 1851 to 1858. He read much and was well informed on general topics. He was a faithful minister.

Asa Pierce
Birth:
1809
Berkshire
Berkshire County,
Massachusetts
Death:
Jun. 1, 1900
Centerburg, Knox County,
Ohio

Burial:
Centerburg Cemetery
Centerburg, Knox County,
Ohio

Pierce, Rev. Asa, son of Orange and Ruth (Heath) Pierce. In 1812 his parents went to Ohio and located in Delaware County. In 1843 he was converted, and in 1846 was ordained by Rev's G. W. and O. E. Baker. His first pastorate was the Second Centerburg Free Will Baptist church, since which time he has preached for a number of churches in central Ohio and in Indiana. Many precious revivals have blessed his ministry and resulted in the organization by him of several churches. In 1830 he was married to Margaret Debold. Four children blessed this union. In 1852 he was married to Catherine Myers

James Jasper Perry
Birth:
Feb. 12, 1884
Martin County,
Kentucky
Death:
Aug. 29, 1928
Lyra, Scioto County, Ohio
Burial:
Vernon Cemetery,
Lyra, Scioto County, Ohio

A Free Will Baptist Minister.

Edwin Pimlott
Birth: April 10, 1853
Smethwick, England
Death: May 9, 1890
Burial:
Ferncliff Cemetery
Springfield
Clark County, Ohio
Plot: Section I lot 77

His father, Rev. Frank Pimlott, whose two sons became ministers were associated in England with the Primitive Methodist. Edwin was converted in 1868, educated at Hillsdale College, Michigan, and ordained on December 28, 1879. He became the pastor of the Breech Grove church, Ohio and about 1883 entered upon the pastor of the church in East Kendall, New York. He was engaging revival work baptized 30 converts.

Bill Pitts
Birth:
Sep. 10, 1931
Death:
Feb. 26, 2003
Columbus,
Franklin County, Ohio
Burial:
Harrison Township
Cemetery,
South Bloomfield,
Pickaway County, Ohio

Rev. Pitts was the founder and longtime pastor of the Greater Columbus Free Will Baptist Church. He was in the ministry for 41 years.

Arnold J Pollard
Birth:
1931
Death:
1985
Burial:
Putnam Chapel Cemetery
Vinton County, Ohio

He was a retired US Air Force Korea and Vietnam veteran and Free Will Baptist minister pastoring the Puritan church for a number of years.

James Thompson Pollock
Birth:
1834
Death:
Apr. 29, 1917
Ohio
Burial:
Woodland Cemetery and
Arboretum
Dayton
Montgomery County, Ohio

POLLOCK, Rev. J. T. (may be the one on list?) 1834-1917, OH. He was m. to Elizabeth A. Andrews, 12 June 1867, OH; Children: Frances (Fannie), 1868, OH; Margaret R, 11 March 1870, Osborn, Greene Co. OH; infant son: C. Freddie, 07 Jan-1872; Melville, b. 14 Mar. 1876, Tiffin, Seneca, OH. James Thompson POLLOCK, served as Chap. in Civil War, Indiana 96th Inf. Drew pension in 1897 until he d. 1917.

R. P. Porter
Birth:
1821
Death:
1883
Burial:
Mount Tabor Cemetery,
Huntington Township,
Gallia County, Ohio

The Harrisburg Freewill Baptist Church was organized April 4, 1862 with Porter being one of the organizing ministers. He was later a it's pastor.

Raymond Sebastian Powers
Birth: Mar. 6, 1921
Virginia
Death:
Oct. 23, 1982
Norwalk, Huron County, Ohio

Burial:
Mount Hope Cemetery
Shiloh
Richland County, Ohio

He died from an apparent heart attack at the Crestview-Edison in football game in Milan, Ohio. He moved to Mansfield, Ohio in 1955 and then to Shiloh in 1962. He had been a clerk at the Empire-Detroit Steel Company since 1955. He was a Past Master of the Shiloh Masonic Lodge number 542 and Past Patron of the Shiloh Eastern Star number 322. He held the Knights Templar degree. He was ordained to the ministry in 1949 for the Free Will Baptist denomintion. He served with the United States Army Air Force from 1940 to 1945. Services were held at the Wesley Evangelical church in Shiloh by the Rev. Carlos Allen Junior of the Clear Creek Church of Christ, Ashland.

Cecil William Price
Birth:
Mar. 27, 1927
Gallia County, Ohio
Death:
Jan. 6, 1991
Jackson, Ohio
Burial:
Gravel Hill Cemetery,
Cheshire, Gallia County, Ohio

He was a US Navy and Army World War II veteran who retired from the Ohio Valley Electric Corporation at Kyger Creek. He was a member of the Old Kyger Free Will Baptist Church near Cheshire. He was also a Free Will Baptist preacher.

Pemberton Randall
Birth:
Oct. 6, 1807
Lebanon
New London County,
Connecticut
Death:
Jan. 4, 1891
Minneapolis
Hennepin County, Minnesota
Burial:
Spring Grove Cemetery
Medina
Medina County, Ohio
Plot: section 2 lot 97

Medina County Gazette- January 9, 1891: Pemberton Randall - in his book entitled *"The Wonderful Tent"*, Rev. D. A. Randall, D. D., is written, and from which we learn that "Rev. Pemberton Randall was one of seven children born to James Randall and his wife, Joanna Pemberton Randall. The parents were able to bestow upon their children little less than those born with good blood and Christian influences. The Randall's originated in bonnie Scotland, in this stirring annual of which County the family name is not obscure. The Pemberton's sprang from sturdy English stock, possessed of both ability and nobility. Joanna was a direct descendent of Ebenezer Pemberton, D. D., one of the early distinguished pastors of Old South Church, Boston. Both father and mother were native New Englanders. Rev. Pembleton Randall departed this life at the home of his daughter, with whom he and his wife were living. Mrs. Sarah) A. R. (Randall) McGeah, in

Minneapolis, Minnesota, at about eight o'clock on Sunday morning, January 4, 1891, being a little past 84 years of age. He was born in Lebanon, Connecticut. In early life, in fact in the autumn of 1826, he and his brother, Rev. Austin Randall, D. D., embraced the Christian religion in a revival meeting held by Rev. David Marks, a Free Will Baptist revivalist who came to a neighboring church and began a series of meetings. In addition to attending the meetings for some three weeks, he and his brothers, alone or in concert, engaged daily in Scripture readings, praying or in meditation. Both made a public profession of religion and on the day before Christmas, by Elder Haskell, pastor of the local church, baptized into Canandaigua Lake. Pemberton adopted the doctrine of the revivalist, and in due time became a cultivated and conscientious minister of the Free Will Church.

Soon after his conversion he removed to Ohio, and after receiving a common school education, he pursued a classical course for two years in Geauga Seminary.

In 1840 he was ordained by Elders Cyrus Coltrim and Warmer Beebe. His labors was with churches in northern Ohio. He has an able preacher, his sermons being clear, logical and strong arguments in favor of the religion of Christ. Young ministers have always considered it a great privilege to listen to his preaching, and although over 80 years of age his mental powers were clear and strong, and the Free Will Baptist Quarterly Meetings were often blessed with his presence and counsel. In February 1834 he was joined in marriage to Maria T. Beebe, who died in February, 1839, and in 1840 he was married to Sarah C. Foster. He was the father of 10 children; five of whom and his wife survived him.

He was regarded as one of the strongest intellectual scriptural preachers of the denomination, and of which he was a worthy and honored member.

His membership was transferred from Spencer, Ohio, to the Free Will Baptist church of Minneapolis, Minnesota, where his wife is also a member. He was able to converse intelligently to the last, and died trusting in Jesus for the life of one which he has entered in the immortality of the glory world.

His remains in Medina, Ohio

on Wednesday morning was, accompanied by his wife and son in law, Mr. J. A. McGeagh, and the funeral services were Thursday afternoon at 2 PM, in Medina in the Baptist church, conducted by Rev. G. H. Damon and assisted by resident and other ministers of other denominations.

He was a bi-vocational Minister and a Free Will Baptist pastor who resided in Scioto County, Ohio for 40 years. As a Free Will Baptist pastor he served the Sciotodale, Bloom, Antioch and Owl Creek churches; Sciotodale Baptist and the Fallen Timber Christian church. He was a retired Detroit Steel Corp. He was a member of the Scioto Valley Ministerial Association.

Earl E. Rankin
Birth:
Sep. 14, 1897
Olive Hill,
Carter County,
Kentucky
Death:
Jan., 1970
Portsmouth,
Scioto County Ohio
Burial:
Salisbury Cemetery
Stockdale,
Pike County,
Ohio

John Robert Reese
Birth:
May 11, 1921
Death:

Jun. 18, 1993
Ohio
Burial:
Buffalo Cemetery
Buffalo
Guernsey County, Ohio

Churches Pastored: Hickory Grove Baptist Church, Oak Hill, Ohio; Germany Hollow Free Will Baptist, Wheelersburg, Ohio; Buckeye Free Will Baptist Church, Jackson, Ohio; Coalton Free Will Baptist Church, Coalton, Ohio; Buffalo Free Will Baptist Church, Buffalo, Ohio. As well as being an evangelist for several years.

David Lyman Rice
Birth:
May 1, 1820, Green, Ohio
Death:
Nov. 19, 1886
Burial:
Westwood Cemetery
Oberlin
Lorain County, Ohio
Plot: H-001-03A

His father resided for a while in Québec but shortly after settled in Ohio before 1820. David was converted in 1834 and baptized the following March by Reverent Ransom Dunn.

His education was obtained at Geauga Seminary. He was licensed by the Green church in 1843 and ordained by the Ashtabula Quarterly Meeting at Lenox on May 17, 1846. After a pastoring a number of churches, he entered another work as an agent for Hillsdale College in 1855. He continued this work until 1876 traveling among the churches conducting revivals and instructing the people as to the needs of the college and its importance to the denomination. In all he gathered more than $50,000 for the endowment of the college and at the same time turning the footsteps of many young men and women toward classic calls and higher life. In 1877 he became pastor of the church at Pierpoint, Ohio and then in 1884 the Burgh church. He is buried in the same Cemetery as the famous Charles Finney and Free Will Baptist leader David Marks.

Melford William Riddlebarger
Birth:
Oct. 10, 1906
Scioto County, Ohio
Death:
Nov. 27, 2003 Portsmouth, Scioto County, Ohio
Burial:
Memorial Burial Park, Wheelersburg, Scioto County, Ohio

He pastored in southern Ohio and was popular among the churches in the area.

Russell Homer Risner
Birth:
Mar. 20, 1934
Death:
Sep. 23, 1987
Burial:
Preston Cemetery, Alger, Hardin County, Ohio

James Richard Roby
Birth:
Jul. 1, 1977
Bellefontaine, Logan County, Ohio
Death:
Aug. 14, 2011
Bellefontaine, Logan County,, Ohio
Burial:
Greenwood Cemetery
De Graff, Logan County, Ohio

Rev. James Richard Roby, 57, of De Graff, was a son of Richard Wilbur Roby of De Graff and the late Shirley Joanne Vaughn Roby. On September 23, 1977, he married Debra Diane Kendall in Bellefontaine.
He was a 1972 graduate of Riverside High School and a graduate of Urbana College. He was the Pastor at the De Graff Freewill Baptist Church.

Rev Ferrell M. Rood

Birth:
Jun. 13, 1937
Huntington
Cabell County, West Virginia
Death:
Dec. 4, 2015
Chillicothe
Ross County, Ohio
Burial
Oak Grove Cemetery
Zaleski, Vinton County, Ohio

Pastor Ferrell M. Rood, age 78 of Zaleski, passed away at the Adena Regional Medical Center in Chillicothe, Ohio. He was born in Huntington, W.Va. to the late Perry U. Rood and Lillie A. Shaver Rood. Ferrell was a 1955 graduate of Wellston High School. He was the Pastor of the Zaleski Free Will Baptist Church for 20 years, as well as being a self-employed contractor. Ferrell was an avid West Virginia Mountaineer fan, who enjoyed reading and spending time with his family. Funeral Home in Wellston with Brother Mark A. Rood, Jr. officiating.

M. Kenneth Rose

Birth:
Feb. 4, 1932
Emerson, Lewis County, Kentucky
Death:
May 17, 2010
Mansfield, Richland County, Ohio
Burial:
Franklin Cemetery, Mansfield, Richland County, Ohio

Rev David Valoy Ross

Birth:
Sep. 1, 1842
Pennsylvania
Death:
Sep. 6, 1878
Ohio
Burial:
West Woodville Cemetery
Warren County, Ohio

Rev. David V. Ross, was born to William Ross and Amanda Pratt Ross, in Penn. When five years of age with his parents he moved from Pennsylvania to Clermont, OH. In 1861, he entered U.S. military service, and received honorable discharge at end of three years. He began preaching for the Methodists, but joined the Free Baptist in 1876 and was ordained by the Miami Quarterly Meeting the January before his death.

Samuel S Schnell
Birth:
Apr. 22, 1854
Liverpool, Ohio
Death: May 2, 1936
Burial:
Beebe Town Cemetery
Beebetown
Medina County, Ohio

Being converted in 1875, he entered Hillsdale College in 1877 taking the classical course and later at the theological. On September 24, 1883 he was ordained by the Genesee Quarterly Meeting, Michigan, and has since served the churches of Millington and Leslie, Michigan and Lenox, Ohio.

Rev Louis Emory Sealey
BIRTH
unknown
DEATH 1957
BURIAL
Dayton Memorial Park
Cemetery
Dayton, Montgomery County,
Ohio, USA
PLOT   CH AB 6_43 4

Rev Miranda Searl
Birth:
Mar. 14, 1808
Steuben County
New York
Death:
Dec. 19, 1891
Wheelersburg
Scioto County
Ohio
Burial:
South Webster Cemetery
South Webster
Scioto County, Ohio

Rev. Searl was converted in 1834, received license in 1837, and was ordained in April 1843, his connection being with the United Brethren.

In 1857, he united with the Freewill Baptists and has since ministered to the Hamilton, Union, Porter, Madison, Wheelersburg, and Sciotoville churches of the Little Scioto Quarterly Meeting, Ohio. He has baptized about fifty converts.

Rev. Miranda Searl, of Iron Furnace, OH, was the son of Nathaniel and Rebecca (White) SEARL.

He was married to Mary Coburn, Jan. 22, 1829.

Rev Jacob Harrell See
Birth:
Aug. 8, 1893
Lawrence County
Kentucky
Death:
Nov. 8, 1967
Portsmouth
Scioto County
Ohio
Burial:
Memorial Burial Park
Wheelersburg
Scioto County
Ohio

Son of William V. and Nancy Jane Kirk See. Married first to Rhoda Frances Meek, who pre-deceased him. His second wife was Della Mae Barker.

He was a Freewill Baptist minister and was retired from Norfolk and Western Railroad as an air inspector and car repairman.

An ordained FWB minister in Ohio, and in the formation of Ohio's State Association, his name appearing with other minister's names who were present.

Rev. Isaac Seitz
Birth:
Aug. 2, 1828
Seneca County, Ohio
Death:
1890
Burial:
Greenlawn Cemetery
Tiffin
Seneca County, Ohio
Plot: Sect C, row
Plot 6, grv 23

Rev. Isaac Seitz was converted in 1866 and united with the Methodist church and in 1875 was licensed as a local preacher. In his studies he changed his doctrinal belief on the question of baptism and other doctrines; and in 1877, he changed his church relations, uniting with the Bloom Free Baptist church. In May 1878, he was ordained by the Seneca and Huron Quarterly Meetings (QM). He has had care of churches in the Marion, and Richland and Licking Q.M's, and organized one church. He has written an interesting book containing an account of

his own experiences; a reply to Ingersoll, and a statement of his doctrinal views as gathered from the word of God. He pastored also the church as Rome, OH.
Note: 1st Sgt Co G 164 OVI

Louis E. Shannon
Birth: 1855
Death: 1924
Burial:
Pleasant Union Cemetery
Old Fort
Seneca County
Ohio
Plot: sec 7 lot 49

Rev. C. Curtis Sheets
Birth
December 10, 1933
Death
June 27, 2017
Cremated

Sheets Rev. C. Curtis Sheets, age 83. He was the pastor of Pleasant View Free Will Baptist Church for 46 years and 5 years in Tampa, Florida.

It later changed its name to Pleasant View Baptist Church. Preceded in death by mother Garnet B. Watson-Sheets and father Carroll R. Sheets. Left to cherish his memory, loving wife of 65 years, Kathryn M. Graham-Sheets; son, Rockie A. Sheets (Loretta); daughters, LuAnne Emrick (Virgil) and Robin Nichols (David); funeral service at Pleasant View Baptist Church, Grove City, Ohio with Rev. John Meade officiating.

William J. Sheppard
Birth:
1881
Death:
1945
Scioto County, Ohio
Burial:
Vernon Cemetery,
Lyra,
Scioto County,
Ohio

Early pastor and Ohio leader in the newly formed Free Will Baptists State re-organization.

Warren Simpkins
Birth:
Sep. 5, 1948
Paintsville,
Kentucky
Death:
Mar. 15, 2010
Commercial Point
Pickaway County,
Ohio
Burial:
Beckett Cemetery
Commercial Point
Pickaway County,
Ohio

He was the assistant pastor at the Mt. Sterling Free Will Baptist Church where he also taught the Young Adult Sunday School and was the head of the Youth Olympics for the Trinity Conference. He was active in the Courthouse Manor Nursing Home services and sang in the Lighthouse Singers Quartet.

Rev Jesse C "Jessie" Sizemore
Birth:
Nov. 4, 1888
Death:
Mar. 11, 1954
Burial:
Puckett Cemetery
Pedro
Lawrence County, Ohio
Father: James Sizemore b: 01 MAY 1848 & Mother: Sarah Henry b: MAR 1852
He was a minister in the Free WIll Baptist, and was elected assistant moderator of the Ohio State Association in 1939. Other information concerning his ministry is unavailable. Spouse: Hattie Delawder Sizemore (1891 - 1968).

Jacob Shonkwiler
Birth:
May 1, 1805
Scioto County, Ohio
Death:
Dec. 18, 1882
Lucasville
Scioto County, Ohio
Burial:
Owl Creek Cemetery,
Beaver, Pike County, Ohio

He was one of the earliest Free Will Baptist ministers in southern Ohio and especially in Scioto County. He was a minister and farmer in this County as well as Pike County, Ohio. He was converted in early life under the labors of Elder Samuel Branch, and was an active minister forty years, having been ordained about 1849. He was connected with the Madison church of the Little Scioto Quarterly Meeting, and labored in this vicinity." --- from "Free Baptist Cyclopedia," pub. 1889, by Burgess and Ward.
Married twice and had five children by each wife. In August of 1841, he was ordained a Free Will Baptist. He was the pastor of the Hamilton Free Will Baptist Church in 1884, which had been organized in 1881 and a church building was erected that same year. The first pastor of this congregation was Isaac Fullerton. Jacob preached in southern Ohio and in Maysville, Kentucky area. He was a rabid abolitionist and became engaged in the abolition movement. Tradition says that he and his cousin the Rev. Isaac Fullerton, helped slaves escape from Kentucky into Ohio then into Canada.

James Ava. Shonkwiler
Birth:
Oct. 7, 1877
Pike County Ohio
Death:
October 21, 1955
Hilliard,
Franklin County, Ohio

Burial:
Owl Creek Cemetery
Pike County, Ohio

He was one of the older of the Free Will Baptist ministers in southern Ohio and was a member of the Owl Creek church which still exists.

Carl R. Sizemore
Birth:
July 17, 1917
Death:
2009
Burial:
Puckett Cemetery, Pedro, Lawrence County, Ohio

Rev. Carl R. Sizemore, 91, of Pedro, Lawrence County, Ohio native was the son of the late Rev, Jesse C. and Hattie Delawder Sizemore. Mr. Sizemore attended Pedro Schools, was a U.S. Army WWII Veteran and a former coal miner for over 40 years with Collins Mining Company. He was a member of Symmes Valley Freewill Baptist Church in Aid, Ohio.

Denver Earl Smith
Birth:
Apr. 8, 1920
Death:
Feb. 14, 1992
Burial:
South Webster Cemetery,

South Webster,
Scioto County, Ohio

Rev Troy W. Smith, Jr
Birth:
Apr. 22, 1944
Death: Apr. 1, 2015
Ohio
Burial:
Fairview Cemetery
Mount Vernon
Knox County, Ohio

Rev. Troy W. Smith, Jr., age 70, of Nebo, went home to be with the Lord Wednesday, April 1, 2015 at Memorial Campus – Mission Hospital. Rev. Smith was born April 22, 1944 and was a son of the late Troy Weaver Smith, Sr. and Annie Jackson Smith. He was a very loving, meek and happy person.. He had grit, and was a hard worker. His family will remember him as a wonderful husband, father, grandfather and great grandfather, brother, brother-in-law and friend to many. He was a great mentor to his children and friends. He pastored numerous churches for 42 years in MI, VA, NC and TN. He proudly served his country in the US Army 82nd Airborne.

Surviving Rev. Smith is his wife of 50 years, Bobbie Jean Smith, of the home; Rodney

Smith, son and wife Melinda of Nebo; Michelle Smith Scoles, daughter and husband Keith of Nebo; two brothers, Jackson Smith and wife Shirley of Candler and Roy Smith and wife Sue also of Candler; three sisters, Claudine Reese and husband Jimmy of Weaverville, Peggy Smith Warren of Leicester and Debbie Brittain and husband Gene of Mills River; nine grandchildren, two great granddaughters and a brother-in-law, Lamar Crisp and wife Sharon of Bostic.

A funeral service was held Saturday, April 4, 2015 at 3:30 pm at Fairview Free Will Baptist church with Revs. Elisha Fish, Ted Reynolds, Terry McDaniel and Scott Hollifield officiating.

Rev. Dr. William L. Snider
Birth:
May 3, 1929
Somerset, Ohio
Death:

February 23, 2020
Burial:
St. Joseph Cemetery
Columbus, Ohio

Rev. Dr. William L. Snider, age 90, was born on to Homer and Nellie Snider. He is preceded in death by his twin brother Joe, brother Robert, and sister Marguerite. Survived by his loving wife of 45 years, Betty J.; sister Loretta; daughter Pamela Richards; sons Rev. Trent Snider and Rev. Michael Gardner.

Dr. Snider graduated from Otterbein University with a Bachelor of Arts degree, Trinity Lutheran Seminary with a Master of Divinity degree, and Slidell Seminary with a Doctor of Theology degree. Dr. Snider was ordained as a minister in 1958 and retired in 2012. In that time, he founded and pastored several churches in the greater Columbus area and touched many lives. He preached with passion and fervor and found no greater joy than leading the lost to Christ.

He served as pastor of churches on the south side of Columbus for over 60 years. A few years ago, he retired as pastor at Good Shepard Community Church on Obetz Rd. Since that time, he and his wife and their families have attended and united in membership with the Heritage Free Will Baptist Church. He has performed more weddings and funerals than any person in Columbus, Ohio. His Clergy records say he conducted over 9000 funerals in the past 68 years. A memorial service was at Heritage Free Will Baptist Church with Dr. Timothy W. Stout, Rev. Brian Humphrey, and Rev. Michael Gardner officiating.

Crate D. Sparks
Birth:
Dec. 18, 1934
Culver,
Elliott County,
Kentucky
Death:
Mar. 16, 2012 Mount
Vernon,
Knox County,
Ohio

Ted B Sowards
Birth:
1905
Death:
1989
Burial:
Friendship Cemetery,
Friendship,
Scioto County,
Ohio

Burial:
Fairview Freewill Baptist
Church Cemetery,
Mount Vernon,
Knox County, Ohio

He began preaching the gospel in 1968. A lifelong servant of God, he founded the Ashley now Victory Freewill Baptist Church. He served the Blooming Grove Freewill Baptist Church, Pleasant Hill Freewill Baptist Church, and founded the Fairview Freewill Baptist Church, where he pastored until 2008. In 1993 he retired from Sunray Stove Company in Delaware, after 33 years of service. A US Navy Veteran, he came to Galena at the age of 18, moved to Mt. Vernon in 1993 and onto Delaware in 2011 to be near his family. Services were held with military honors.

To Live is Christ
To Die is Gain.

Delmar C Sparks
Birth:
Nov. 7, 1927
Death:
Aug. 17, 2002
Estes Park,
Larimer County,
Colorado
Burial:
Blendon Central Cemetery,
Westerville,
Franklin County,
Ohio

He was founder of the Westerville Free Will Baptist Church where he served for 31 years. Besides being an outstanding pastor he was a very active denominational leader. He represented the state of Ohio on the General Board of the National Association from 1984-2002. He was also honored to speak at the national convention in 1989 in Tampa, Florida. As a local pastor he served on many district ordaining council's, mission board and moderator. On the state level he served as the moderator of the state Association, served on the State General Board and Executive Board. His early ministry was among the Enterprise Baptist churches before his leaving to organize the Westerville church in 1959. He was a marvelous mentor and fellow servant.

Asa Stearns
Birth:
Feb. 3, 1782
Death:
Sept. 7, 1851
Mercer County, Ohio
Burial:
Elm Grove Cemetery
Saint Marys
Auglaize County, Ohio

Sophia Higley was married to Asa Stearns, a Free Will Baptist preacher, finally settled in Mercer County, Ohio, where they both died. They had four children, Rufus, Amos, Louise, and Joel. Rufus became a doctor and is buried in the same Cemetery with his mother and father. He was connected with the Meigs Quarterly Meeting in South East Ohio in its early years and saw the fruits of his labor they are because many of the churches and influence still exist. An interesting note appears in the history of Athens County Ohio about how the early ministers were supported. "In the Ames Township area secured to the services of Elder Asa Stearns a pioneer Free Will Baptist preacher to preach for them once a month during the year, to be paid with three barrels of whiskey. Rev. Stearns had an arrangement with Ebenezer Currier, at Athens, to take the whiskey and allow him there for $24 be credited him toward the farm he had bought from Judge Currier. The contract was faithfully carried out on all hands, Elder Stearns visiting the congregation every third Saturday and Sunday of each month during the year at the end of which he received a salary of whiskey and made the transfer he did as agreed to Judge Currier."

Eli Stedman
Birth:
Aug. 17, 1777
Tunbridge,
Orange County, Vermont
Death:
Mar. 28, 1845
Rutland, Meigs County, Ohio
Burial:
Miles Cemetery, Rutland,
Meigs County, Ohio

He came to Ohio in 1804, locating in Belpre, Washington County, but removed to Leading Creek in 1805. He was a preacher of the Free Will Baptist denomination. Elihu Stedman was the youngest child of Eli Stedman and wife. He married Adaline Elliott, daughter of Simeon Elliott, Esq., and a sister of Rev. Madison Elliott, at one time principal of the Chester Academy. Elihu Stedman lived in Middleport many years, but moved to Iowa. Eli started the Old Kyger Free Will Baptist Church in 1805 which is the oldest church in Ohio of this denomination which still exists.

James Oliver Stevens
Birth:
Death:
June 30, 2018
Columbus, Ohio
Burial: Harrison Township Cemetery
South Bloomfield, Ohio

Reverend James Oliver Stevens, age 77. Retired from Madison Correctional Facility. Member of South Columbus Freewill Baptist Church where he was the assistant pastor for many years. Reverend Tim Stevens officiating.

Hertis Stone
Birth:
Jul. 30, 1932
Olive Hill,
Carter County, Kentucky
Death:
Sep. 16, 1998
Mansfield, Richland County, Ohio
Burial:
Mansfield Cemetery, Mansfield, Richland, Ohio

Although he was a Kentuckian he spent the majority of his adult life in Ohio, where he retired from the General Motors CPC plant. Brother Stone was pastor of the Wyandotte Free Will Baptist Church of Mansfield for over 20 years. He was the evangelists for the Northern Ohio Free Will Baptist Conference and was a member of the Cuyahoga-Lorain Free Will Baptists Executive conference board. He also pastored churches in Amherst, Ohio; Huntington, Indiana; Buckeye Lake and Fitchville, Ohio Free Will Baptist churches

Jeremiah A. Sutton
Birth:
1847
Symmes Township
Hamilton County, Ohio
Death:
1921
LaRue, Ohio
Burial:
LaRue Cemetery, La Rue
Marion County, Ohio

Rev. Jeremiah Augustus Sutton, LaRue's grand old man, was found dead in bed by his wife. Sunday morning. Death being caused from heart failure. He had been in his usual health Saturday and was to deliver the sermon at the funeral of Mrs. Milton Anderson, near DeCliff, Sunday afternoon. On the desk in Rev, and Mrs. Sutton's room was the obituary, funeral text and notes on the sermon to be used. The service was conducted by Rev. F. E. Hawes, pastor of Fite Memorial Baptist church, of Marion, who used the text chosen by Rev. Mr. Sutton. Rev. Mr. Sutton was perhaps the most widely known minister in the county and to know him was to win a friend in the truest sense of the word. He had long been called the "marrying and burying parson," having delivered 2,089 funeral sermons and performing 746 marriage services. Rev. Mr. Sutton was ordained to the ministry October 24, 1874. He came to Marion County in 1879 accepting the pastorate in Green Camp Baptist church. This position he held until April 8, 1890 when he was appointed chaplain to the Ohio State penitentiary, which position he filled for about two years. During his pastorate in the institution, Rev. Mr. Sutton organized what was known as the Ohio Penitentiary Sunday-school and through his association had eighty-four conversions. In 1894 Rev. Mr. Sutton moved to LaRue, where he served twelve consecutive years as pastor of the Free Will Baptist church. With the exception of a short time passed as pastor of a charge in West Mansfield, he passed the remainder of his life in LaRue. Rev. Mr. Sutton was twice married, the first wife being Miss Mollie Cox, who died November 28, 1869. March 22, 1883, he was married to Mrs. Helen Kniffin..

Rev. Mr. Sutton had held all the offices in the church and a large number of offices in the township and village. He had been a notary public for the past thirty-one years, and at the time of his death was clerk of Montgomery Township. At one time he was editor of the LaRue News.

Rev Lawson C. Swaim
Birth:
Apr. 16, 1846
Scioto County
Ohio
Death:
Nov. 7, 1900
Burial:
Buchtel Cemetery
Buchtel
Athens County, Ohio

Rev. Lawson C. Swaim, son of

George W. Swaim, was born in Scioto Co. Ohio. He was converted at the age of twenty-three years and began preaching soon after, but was not ordained until 1878. The most of his time has been devoted to evangelist labor and several hundred persons have been converted under his preaching and baptized by him. He has organized four churches and was pastor at Madison and Scioto. In March, 1866, He was married to Feemelia Woodruff.

Brighton N Tanner
Birth:
1852
Chester, Ohio
Death:
Apr. 1, 1932

Burial:
Lake View Cemetery
Cleveland
Cuyahoga County, Ohio
Plot: Section 42 Lot 782-0

He was educated at Geauga, Ohio. In 1885 he consecrated his life to God and May 20, 1888 was licensed to preach by the Geauga and Portage Quarterly Meeting.

Rev Fred Thomas Taylor
Birth
26 Feb 1932
North Carolina
Death
14 Jun 1993
Perrysburg,
Wood County, Ohio
Burial
Fort Meigs Cemetery
Perrysburg,
Wood County, Ohio
Plot   Block 008
Site Num.10B Lot 004

He was pastor for many years in Toledo, Ohio and had a radio ministry for most of his service to the church called the Country Parson.

Inscription
Korea A2C USAF b.Marion SC
Cntry Parsn

Paul Elden Taylor
Birth:
Aug. 18, 1921
Cheshire,
Gallia County, Ohio
Death:
Dec. 20, 2004
Rutland, Meigs County, Ohio
Burial:
Gravel Hill Cemetery,
Cheshire, Gallia County, Ohio

Rev. Taylor served as pastor to the Rutland Freewill Baptist Church for 30 years and he shared his ministry for 12 years in Utah. During World War II he served four years in the U.S. Army in the Philippines as a foot soldier.

Rev Merlin Eldridge Teets

Birth:
Jan. 25, 1920
Braxton, West Virginia
Death:
March 6, 1993
Columbus, Franklin Co., Ohio
Burial:
Glen Rest Memorial Estate
Reynoldsburg
Franklin County, Ohio
Plot: Section B

He was raised in a Christian home, the fourth of five children born to Cleova and Leota (Helmick) Teets of Braxton County, West Virginia.

In 1942 he met Ida Stout at a cottage prayer meeting. They were married June 9, 1943. Shortly after he enlisted in the army for the duration of the war plus six months. He was sent to France.

The year 1949 a revival was held at Eureka Methodist Church where they attended with his family during his years at home. Shortly after they were saved, they moved back to Cabin Creek, West Virginia where he went to work in the coal mines. During that time, he met and joined a group of men who formed a quartet. They traveled to various churches to minister through song.. During those years he was feeling a strong call from God to preach. In 1949 he surrendered to that call.

He did trial preaching in many area churches and denominations. After studying the doctrines of many churches, he came to believe the tenets of the Free Will Baptist Association most closely mirrored his understanding of the scriptures. He was ordained by the Free Will Baptist Association. Although he was an ordained FWB preacher, he never turned down an opportunity to share the unfiltered gospel of Christ in any church, regardless of their denomination. His preaching ministry spanned six states and some 15 denominations.

In addition to his pastorates, he had a vibrant and effective evangelistic and radio ministry. He did a live half-hour program on WMPO Middleport, Ohio every Sunday afternoon. While he was the Ohio state Evangelist he had a weekly program in Jackson, Ohio. During good weather he would set up his big tent and hold tent revivals wherever he felt a call, and had an opportunity to go. He pastored the following churches: Mt. Union FWB Church, The Plains, FWB Church Silver Run FWB Church, Zaleski FWB Church,

Woodland Chapel FWB (twice) First FWB Church (formerly Belmont Baptist Church, Puritan FWB Church, and the Wellston FWB Church. After retiring helped with the revitalization of a number of churches. He had a great love and burden for people and worked in churches until he became physically unable to serve. He held the following known positions during his ministry: Promotional Secretary for State of Ohio, Ohio State Evangelist, and was the third Editor of "The Ambassador," a denominational state publication. He was a featured speaker at the 47th annual Ohio State Association.

Most of his record books were lost, but in an old one that was found, a compilation of this record showed that for August 1953 through August 1963 (nine years, he preached 2,185 sermons, held 83 revivals, and saw 812 people give their life to Christ. These numbers do not include those in the unfound record books, nor include the marriages or funerals that he preached, or the number of baptisms he conducted.

His ministry spanned over 44 years. He wrote, "I feel God has called me to preach His word, and woe is me if I preach not this gospel." He had the God-given ability to present God's word in an effective, compelling manner. He was privileged to start two churches and assist in starting three others, all of which are still thriving churches. He also had a deep appreciation and love for the young ministers who had received the call to preach and mentored many. Jim Eberts preached his funeral. His message was "Who Will Carry the Torch?"

Clyde Thompson, Jr
Birth:
Mar. 28, 1939
Grahn, Carter County, Kentucky
Death:
May 2, 2012
Mansfield, Richland County, Ohio
Burial:
Mound Cemetery, Piketon, Pike County, Ohio

He was a veteran of the United States Army and had retired from Wickes Lumber

Company after driving a truck for over 30 years. He was a Free Will Baptist minister having pastored churches in Ohio and Indiana. He was a member of the Dean Road Free Will Baptist Church in Mansfield, Ohio.

Rev Robert Barry Thompson
Birth:
Nov. 18, 1944
Logan County
West Virginia
Death:
Jan. 30, 2015
Cheshire
Gallia County, Ohio
Burial:
Gravel Hill Cemetery
Cheshire
Gallia County, Ohio

He was son of the late Okey and Inez Thompson, and was the youngest of twelve children.

Bob was the Pastor of Old Kyger Freewill Baptist Church. He worked as a meat cutter in the D.C., Maryland and Beckley, WV area, and retired as the meat manager of Save-A-Lot in Pomeroy, Ohio. He loved preaching, serving, and doing work for the Lord since 1980. He pastored several churches in West Virginia, Tempa Baptist, Kilsyth FWB, and Odd FWB. Bob enjoyed vacationing at the beach, riding his motorcycle, fishing, and loved reading and talking about eagles. He served in the U.S. Navy during the Vietnam Era. Bob was married to Opal in Upper Marlboro, Maryland on August 26, 1966.

**Live For Eternity
God Esteems And Calls**

Samuel Titus
Birth:
1796
Northumberland County
Pennsylvania
Death:
Feb. 18, 1859
Harrison Furnace, Scioto
County, Ohio
Burial:
Titus Cemetery
Minford, Scioto County, Ohio

He married 15 Jul 1816 Ontario Co, New York, Clarrisa Coryell. Son of: Tetus Titus 1755-1765 Montgomery Co, NY who died in 1825 at Scioto Co, Ohio. His mother was Polly Johnson B: Unknown who died in 1819 at Madison Twps., Scioto Co, Ohio 1884). He was the first pastor of the Harrison FWB church of Minford, Ohio.

Miles Lee Trout
Birth:
Sep. 17, 1922
Gallipolis,Gallia County

Ohio
Death:
Sep. 8, 2013
Cheshire
Gallia County, Ohio
Burial:
Ohio Valley Memory Gardens
Gallipolis
Gallia County
Ohio

He was a retired supervisor of the Columbus Southern Power Co. He also was the pastor of several Free Will Baptists churches, and was a member of the Silver Memorial FWB church, the Gallia County Ministerial Association, and the Gallia Quarterly Conference. He was a World War II veteran having served in the U.S. Army Air Corp. Son of James W. and Nell Board Trout. He was married to Ada E. Saunders Trout and second to Helen A. Shuler Trout.

Alvin Trusty
Birth:
1918
Death:
1955
Burial:
Preston Cemetery, Alger,
Hardin County, Ohio
Plot: Section 2
(East), row 18

Charles Alexander Twining
Birth:
May 23, 1821
Hunterdon County
New Jersey
Death:
Dec. 21, 1903
Kipton
Lorain County
Ohio
Burial:
Camden Cemetery
Kipton, Lorain County, Ohio

Charles Alexander Twining, one of the most prosperous and wealthy of the prominent farmers of Henrietta Township.

Samuel Twining, father of subject, was born Feb. 22, 1796, in Hunterdon County, N. J., and moved his family to Broome County, N. Y., in 1823, where he died April 10, 1831. On September 23, 1815, he married Elizabeth Stout, who died October 17, 1882. Her people were wealthy, but on the death of her parents she lost all that she became heiress to. Samuel was a farmer, miller, cloth dresser and distiller; and at the time of his death owned fifty acres of land near Binghamton, N. Y. He left five children, a mother-in-law and sister-in-law for our subject to assist in providing for, and, although the latter was but ten years old when his father died, he was the '"main spoke in the wheel."

Charles A. Twining, whose name opens this sketch, received but a limited education at the subscription schools of the place of his nativity. On October 18, 1842, he was married. by Squire Jesse Richards, to Miss Nellie Schermerhorn, and for about seven years thereafter they continued to reside in Broome county, N. Y. In 1840 they came to Lorain County, Ohio, and Mr. Twining, having saved some five hundred dollars from his earnings, bought a small piece of land in Pittsfield Township, Lorain County, where he resided three years. At the end of this time he sold out to his three brothers and returned to Broome County, N. Y., where he bought the old home farm formerly owned by his father. After residing here three years he sold out, returned to Ohio, and bought a farm in Camden Township, Lorain County. Sold this farm and bought in Russia Township; sold this and bought a farm in Henrietta Township, which he still owns. In 1888 he built a comfortable modern dwelling, situated in Henrietta Township. and his property has increased from time to time till he now owns 720 acres of prime farm land, divided into seven farms, with good buildings. He has owned farms in Brownhelm and West Henrietta, and in Erie County, in Florence Township; three farms in West Clarksfield, Huron County, Brighton Township, Lorain County, and Wakeman, Huron County, and resided on all of these except the one in Wakeman. He has given his daughter Sarah Ann a good farm in Camden Township, and has settled his six living sons on good farms, and has also dealt quite extensively in livestock.

Eleven children were born to Mr. and Mrs. Twining,

The entire family are members of the Freewill Baptist Church, except Perry, who is a member of the Methodist Church, and all brought up in the path of Christian rectitude, which they have in no instance deviated from. The sons have never used liquor or tobacco in any form. Mr. Twining in his political affiliations has always been a staunch Democrat, and has served his county to the best of his ability, and held offices of trust. Mr. Twining formerly belonged to the Methodist Church, where he was class-leader and superintendent of Sabbath schools for a number of years, and also held an exhorter's license. In 1866 Mr. Twining spent one year with his family in Ocean county, N.J., stopping at a pleasure resort in Point Pleasant.

(Source: Commemorative Biographical Record of the Counties of Huron and Lorain, Ohio, Chicago, Beers and Co., 1894.)

F. A. Twining
Birth:
Jun. 30, 1866
Florence
Erie County
Ohio
Death:
Jan. 7, 1945
Hiram
Portage County
Ohio
Burial:
Camden Cemetery
Kipton
Lorain County
Ohio
Plot: Section A - 44D West

Information from Ohio Death Cert. Occupation, retired minister.
Parents: Charles Alexander Twining (1821 - 1903) Nellie Schermerhorn Twining (1824 - 1907) Spouse:
Carrie M Hardy Twining (1873 - 1961)

Former Marion Pastor Stricken

REV. F. A. TWINING

Rev. F. A. Twining, 79, a former pastor of Fife Memorial Baptist church, died in his home at Hiram, O., yesterday. He died as the result of a stroke of paralysis. He had suffered previous strokes.

A native of Oberlin, he held Baptist pastorates at Coshocton, Canton, Green Camp and Marion. He was pastor at Green Camp from April, 1905 to October, 1907. In 1913 he served the Fife Memorial congregation when the organization was yet in the form of a mission Sunday school, then again for two years when it was an established church, about 15 years ago.

The widow, Mrs. F. A. Twining, survives. A daughter, Mrs. Ruth Whitcomb is a librarian at Hiram college, Hiram, O., and a son, Arthur, some time ago located in Iowa. Three grandchildren survive also, one of whom, a grandson, is in service.

William Tracy Twining

Birth:
Sep. 4, 1847
New York
Death:
Sep. 22, 1936
Henrietta
Lorain County
Ohio
Burial:
Camden Cemetery
Kipton
Lorain County
Ohio

William was a retired Farmer. Son of Alex Twining.

His Death Certificate lists him as Married to Clara Twining.

W. T. Twining. The Twining family has been represented in Lorain County for nearly sixty-five years. W. T. Twining is now living practically retired in Henrietta Township but for many years was engaged in the vigorous prosecution of his business as a general farmer, dairyman and stockman. The name is one that has always been associated with honorable citizenship and a substantial influence in behalf of community welfare.

A native of New York State, W. T. Twining was born September 4, 1847, a son of Charles A. and Nellie (Schermerhorn) Twining. The Twining family is of old American ancestry, and the first of the name was William Twining who came from England and settled on the Atlantic coast soon after 1630. Grandfather Samuel Twining was born February 22, 1796, and followed the business of farmer and miller, making his home in Broome County, New York. In that county he was married in 1813 to Elizabeth Stout.

Charles A. Twining was born in New York State April 23, 1821 and died December 21, 1903. His wife was born in the same state October 8, 1824, and died in 1907. Charles A. Twining, so long known as one of the most successful men of Lorain County, started life with absolutely nothing, and for a number of years had to support not only his sisters but his mother and stepfather. At the time of his death his estate included over 500 acres of land. He first came to Ohio in 1849, but it was in 1852 that he made permanent settlement in Lorain County. He brought to this county $500 and with that as capital purchased his first land in Pittsfield Township. Later he bought a farm in Camden Township and still later in Henrietta Township, in which locality he lived until his death. He became a prominent stock raiser and also dealt extensively in lands, and at one time owned eight different farms. Charles A. and Nellie Twining were married in 1842 and of their eight children seven are still living: Sarah Ann, widow of LeGrand Gibson, and living at Clarksfield. Ohio; W. T.; Gertrude Elizabeth, now deceased; Alvah F. of Henrietta Township; Floyd Odell of Henrietta Township; Virgil Leroy, who has gained success in the hotel business and is now owner of four different hotels and lives at Maumee. Ohio: Perry Eugene, a farmer in Maryland; and Fred A., who is a minister of the Regular Baptist Church, at Coshocton, Ohio. The parents were members of the Free Will Baptist Church, and the father was a democrat in politics.

W. T. Twining gained his early education in the public schools. He worked for his father on the farm until gaining his majority, and was then married to Miss Drucilla Ann Bulkley. They have lived together and worked out their destinies for almost a half a century. Mrs. Twining was a daughter of Jeremiah and Mary Ann (Vincent) Bulkley. Her father was born in New York State September 12, 1824, and died October 20, 1908, and her mother was born in Canada August 8, 1825, and died December 7, 1905. The Bulkley family came to Lorain County in pioneer times and the grandfather and father of Mrs. Twining cleared up a large acreage of land in this section. The Vincent's were also early settlers in Henrietta Township. From "A Standard History of Lorain County "by Geo Frederick Wright.

(1854 - 1923)*
Floyd Odell Twining (1856 - 1939)*
Virgil L Twining (1859 - 1941)*
Fred A Twining (1866 - 1945)*

Francis Tufts
Birth:
Feb., 1743
Medford, Mass.
Death:
Oct. 2, 1833
Warren County, Ohio
Burial:
Maineville Cemetery,
Maineville,
Warren County, Ohio, Plot:
Sec.E

Benjamin Tufts
Birth:
Feb. 12, 1777
Maine
Death:
Aug. 27, 1849
Maineville
Warren County, Ohio
Burial:
Maineville Cemetery
Maineville
Warren County, Ohio

He was converted in 1802 and became connected with the church in Phillips, Maine where he was ordained in 1822. The same year he moved to Ohio where he united with the Maineville Free Will Baptist Church, Hamilton County, and continued to preach as opportunity presented going as far west as Indiana.

Tufts was a true pioneer. He was born in Medford, Mass., but as Maine and Mass. were one large area, he moved from Medford, MA to Farmington, Maine, and was an early contributor to that area.

He served Maine in the Revolutionary War, enlisting in 1775-1777, in Lincoln Co. Maine. He finally received a pension shortly before his death. Where and when he was ordained was associated with the Farmington Q.M., when it was dealing with Rev. Edward Lock on the subject of open communion before

1800, and the votes came out yeas for Rev. Tufts to have open communion. Rev. Moses Dudley (of Maine) had moved to Ohio from Maine, served in the ministry and meetings in this area. They are both buried in this cemetery. (Maineville history states that in 1850 this name was adopted because so many citizens had migrated there from Maine). When Samuel Knowlton, a kinsman friend was removing there, Rev. Francis Tufts (at 87 yrs of age) decided to ride horse-back the one-thousand-mile trip with them to get there. They started Sept. 1, 1831, and arrived Oct 13, 1831, went through nine states, stopping only for "the Sabbath" to worship. Rev. Tufts was always invited to preach which he ably did. It was reported he had a retentive memory--well versed in Old and New Testaments that he could quote entire chapters or suitable portions of scripture. Rev. Tufts was in near perfect physical conditions, but two years later, he passed away. *"The Story of His Predecessors and Descendants"* by Marion Thomas Whitney, pub. 1995, states that Josiah Tufts (1780-1841), who mar. Jane (Greely) Tufts, was his son. Jane was dau. Of Seth Greely (1737-1825) who came to Maineville in 1815.

John F. Tufts
Birth:
Oct. 7, 1829
Barrington
Strafford County, New Hampshire
Death:
May 13, 1873
Warren County, Ohio
Burial:
Maineville Cemetery
Maineville, Warren County, Ohio

His service was among the churches of the Miami Quarterly Meeting. He received license to preach the gospel about 1846 when connected with the Rossbourgh for church and was ordained about three years later. He spent some time at the biblical school in Whitestown, New York. He was a prominent man and much loved in the Miami Quarterly Meeting where he had long service and, noble, and Christian example causing him to be liked by others. He also spent a few years in Iowa. He represented the Ohio Yearly Meeting in the General Conference in 1850.

Clyde Marshall VanHoose
Birth:
Feb. 20, 1933
Johnson County, Kentucky
Death:
Aug. 22, 2011
Burial:
Big Darby Cemetery,
Plain City,
Madison County, Ohio

Employed by Columbus Auto Parts and was the assistant pastor of the North Woodbury Freewill Baptist Church. He was a U.S. Army veteran (1953 to 1955) during the Korean Conflict.

Clovis Vanover
Birth:
Oct. 9, 1933
Laredo, West Virginia
Death:
Columbus, Franklin County, Ohio
Burial:
Mifflin Cemetery,
Gahanna, Franklin County, Ohio

He was the founder and Chairman of the C.W. Vanover Evangelistic Association and a member of the Williams Road FWB Church. He as a State-Wide Evangelist for Ohio Free Will Baptists. He was widely used and well liked.

Rev Kenneth Walker
Birth:
Sep. 18, 1928
Portsmouth, Ohio
Death:
Aug. 20, 2015
Wheelersburg, Ohio
Burial:
Sunset Memorial Gardens
Franklin Furnace
Scioto County, Ohio

Rev. Kenneth Mason Walker, 86, at Best Care Nursing and Rehab Center in Wheelersburg from complications related to cancer. He was born the son of the late Wilburn W. and Dora Frances Arthur Walker. He served in the U.S. Air Force during the Korean Conflict, He was a graduate of Welch College in Nashville and also served as the chairman of its Board of Trustees for 12 years. He established and pastored several Free Will Baptist churches throughout his career, including churches in Washington, D.C., Tulsa, OK, Mobile, AL, Ashland, KY and Deerfield Beach, FL.

His wife, Emma Louise Walker, to whom he was married 68 years; one son, James Stanley Walker, Ph.D; two grandchildren, Dailey and Danner Walker all of Nashville, TN and one brother Walter (Nan) Walker of Waynesville, OH.

A Celebration of Life at the Union Free Will Baptist Church in Wheelersburg with Pastor Chris Oiler, Reverends Dan Widdig and Randy Skaggs officiating.

Rev Francis M. Watkins
Birth: Jul. 18, 1857
Ohio
Death:
Aug. 17, 1927
Burial:
Nye Cemetery
Chauncey
Athens County, Ohio

Ordained Free Baptist minister; son of Wm. T. and Elmira L (Beaman) Watkins. He was ordained in Salem, Ind. Jan. 6, 1889 and pastored

the church there, where he prospered in that work
Inscription:
PVT 119th INF. 50 DIV.
WORLD WAR I VETERAN

Charles H. Webb
Birth:
Mar. 29, 1926
Auxier,
Floyd County, Kentucky
Death:
Mar. 15, 1976
Springdale,
Washington County,
Arkansas
Burial:
Woodlawn Cemetery,
Ada, Hardin County, Ohio

Rev. Charles H. Webb, 49 died at of an apparent heart attack in Springdale Hospital, Springdale, Ark. He was an army veteran of World War II, former pastor of the High Street Freewill Baptist, Rt. 2, Ada, a retired factory worker and member of the High Street Freewill Baptist Church.

Eugene Webb
Birth:
Nov. 5, 1931
Bonanza, Kentucky
Death:
Dec. 10, 2010
Dola, Hardin County, Ohio
Burial:
Dola Cemetery, Dola,
Hardin County, Ohio

Free Will Baptist Minister in western Ohio. He and his wife, Carolyn Yoxsimer Gene was born again on Oct. 12. 1959, in a Freewill Baptist Church and in 1969 he was ordained to preach in the Freewill Baptist Organization. He served as a pastor and assistant pastor. He was a member of the White Oaks Road Freewill Baptist Church, in Marion.

Webb, worked as house parents at the FWB Home for Children in Greeneville, Tn. for three years and later served as a Field Representative for the home in Ohio for three additional years. He served his country in the Korean Conflict from 1951-1953 as a member of the U.S. Army 2nd Division.

Harrison Webb
Birth:
May 4, 1927
Lawrence County, Ohio
Death:
Nov. 28, 2007
Ashland, Boyd County, Kentucky
Burial:
Community Missionary Baptist Church Cemetery, Lawrence County, Ohio

The Lawrence County, Ohio native, the son of the late Simeon and Hazel May Fetters Webb. He is survived by his wife, Maxine Faye Littlejohn Webb, whom he married August 18, 1951. Mr. Webb attended Spring Branch Schools. He was a U.S. Army Korean War Veteran serving from 1948-1952 and received a Bronze Star. He was an iron pourer at the Dayton Malleable Iron Company for 27 years, retiring in 1989. He was a member of Symmes Valley Freewill Baptist Church and was a former pastor at several local churches. He lived in this area all his life.

Simeon J Weed
Birth:
1854
Death:
1927
Burial:
Calvary Baptist Cemetery,
Rio Grande,
Gallia County,
Ohio

Minister, leader, professor at Rio Grande College in Ohio before and after the merger with the Northern Baptists.

John Wheeler
Birth:
Sep. 6, 1787
Rehoboth
Bristol County,
Massachusetts
Death:
Aug. 4, 1879
Greenwich
Huron County, Ohio
Burial:
Steuben Cemetery
Steuben
Huron County, Ohio

In 1805 he married Miss Mary Franklin and moved to Richmond, New York. After serving in the Army of the war of 1812 he was converted and in 1818 moved to Greenfield, Ohio where he began to preach, gathered a church and received ordination in September 1825. After the church was put up on a good basis he resigned the pastorate and labored in that region of the country becoming a circuit preacher helping to found several Free Will Baptist Churches. He had two marriages to the following ladies: Huldah Gregory Wheeler Mary Franklin Wheeler.

Inscription:
Rev. John Wheeler
Died Aug 4, 1879
Aged 90 years 11 months

Billy Joe White

Birth:
May 8, 1941
Logan,
Logan County,
West Virginia
Death:
Aug. 11, 2009
Sullivan,
Ashland County, Ohio
Burial:
Southview Cemetery,
Sullivan,
Ashland County,
Ohio

Billy Joe worked at the Ford Motor Co. in Brook Park for many years, retiring as a general foreman. A man of faith, Billy Joe had served as the pastor of the Free Will Baptist Church in Wellington since 1985. He enjoyed farming.

Philander E. Whittier

Birth:
Aug. 8, 1834
Death:
Oct. 2, 1871
Ohio
Burial:
Cheshire Cemetery
Delaware
Delaware County,
Ohio

Rev. Philander Ellis WHITTIER, was the son of John and Loerza Whittier. He was converted in early life, and after various journeying's [lived in Wisconsin], he married in 1863, in Farmington, ME to Mary Parker Tuffs, and soon settled in Ohio. He was licensed to preach by the Richland and Licking Quarterly Meeting in May 1877, and devoted himself to the work of the ministry with good acceptance, but the end of his labors came soon after.

David Widdig

Birth:
Mar. 17, 1906
Springs,
Sciotoville,
Scioto County, Ohio
Death:
Nov. 16, 1993
Huntington, Cabell
County, West Virginia
Burial:
Memorial Burial Park,
Wheelersburg,
Scioto County,
Ohio

He was a retired electrician employed by the Goodyear Atomic Corporation and was a Free Will Baptist Minister for more than 50 years pastoring four churches.

Marion Wilburn
Birth:
1891
Death:
1951
Scioto County, Ohio
Burial:
South Webster Cemetery,
South Webster,
Scioto County,
Ohio

Alvin Gardner Wilder
Birth:
Nov. 22, 1828
Chesterfield
Hampshire County,
Massachusetts
Death:
Aug. 27, 1875
Berea, Cuyahoga County,
Ohio
Burial:
Beebe Town Cemetery
Beebetown, Medina County,
Ohio

Wilder died at aged 46 years. The family moved to Ohio in 1833 and ten years later Brother Wilder was converted, uniting with the Hinckley church. He was ordained Oct. 5, 1856, by a council from the Medina Q. M. His labors were chiefly with the Hinckley, Royalton, Rockport, Liverpool, and Henrietta churches, and in most of them there remained living evidences of the fruit of his labors.

Charlie Wiley
Birth:
Nov. 29, 1929
Stirrat, Logan County,
West Virginia
Death:
Dec. 8, 2010
Columbus,
Franklin County,
Ohio
Burial:
Glen Rest Memorial Estate,
Reynoldsburg,
Franklin County,
Ohio

Allen Williams, Jr
Birth:
Jan. 9, 1929
Scioto County, Ohio
Death:
Mar. 26, 1996,

Ashland,
Boyd County, Kentucky
Burial:
Clapboard Cemetery,
Franklin Furnace,
Scioto County,
Ohio

He was a son of Allen Williams, Sr and Hazel Ruth Chamberlain. He was a former employee of the Williams Manufacturing Company with 25 years of service. He retired as an employee of Martin Marietta and was a Korean War veteran. He was ordained as a minister in the June, 1957 and served as a pastor of the Pine Creek, Union, Mount Hope and Germany Hollow churches.

Paul Eugene Williams
Birth:
Dec. 8, 1957
Portsmouth,
Scioto County,
Ohio
Death:
Jul. 26, 2010
Portsmouth
Scioto County,
Ohio
Burial:
Bennett Cemetery,
Minford,
Scioto County, Ohio

He was the pastor at Frederick Free Will Baptist Church. Along with Frederick Free Will Baptist Church, he served as pastor at Swauger Valley Free Will, Bloom Free Will, Tick Ridge Free Will and Harvest Chapel Church in Sciotoville. He was a bookkeeper for E.E. Blair Construction Co. in Wheelersburg, and had worked as a bookkeeper for Colonial Florists, Reynolds Bordan and Chapman Accountants in Portsmouth, and the Nancy Rae Supermarket in Wheelersburg. He was a graduate of Minford High School in the class of 1976, and he was very active in the ministry and work of the Free Will Baptist Denomination.

Joe M. Wireman
Birth:
Sep. 10, 1927
Magoffin County,
Kentucky
Death:
Burial:
Fairmont Cemetery,
Uniopolis,
Auglaize County, Ohio

The Rev. Wireman retired from Boilermakers Local 85 in 1990. He was a member of the Cridersville Church, where he was pastor in previous years and continued to minister throughout his life. He has been a faithful and active member of the church for 58 years.

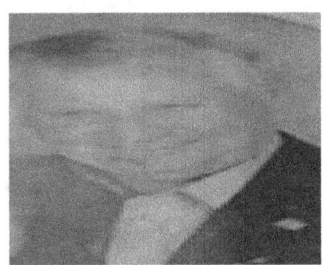

Leslie Wireman
Birth:
Nov. 14, 1932
Death:
Jan. 22, 2007
Alger,
Hardin County, Ohio
Burial:
Preston Cemetery,
Alger,
Hardin County,
Ohio

Floyd I. Wolfenbarger
Birth:
Feb. 16, 1949
Springfield,
Clark County, Ohio
Death:
May 22, 1985
Little Rock,
Pulaski County, Arkansas
Burial:
Vale Cemetery, Springfield,
Clark County, Ohio

A Free Will Baptist minister, writer and denominational leader. He attended Free Will

Baptist Bible College, Oklahoma Bible College, Ohio State University and Cedarville College. Called to preach at age 12 and ordained to the ministry at age 20. He pastored in Oklahoma, Ohio and Arkansas. He was moderator of the Ohio State Association of Free Will Baptists for four years and served eight years as Ohio's General Board Member to the National Association of Free Will Baptists. Six of those years he was a member of the Executive Committee. He wrote articles printed in the *Contact* and *Ambassador Magazines*. A respected leader and minister by his peers.

Andrew Workman
Birth:
Jul. 25
Wayne County,
West Virginia,
Death:
Jun. 21
Portsmouth,
Scioto County, Ohio
Burial:
Evergreen Union Cemetery
Waverly, Pike County ,Ohio

Rev. Workman was known throughout the tri-state area of Ohio, Kentucky, and West Virginia as a Free Will Baptist evangelist and preacher. He was short in stature but tall in evangelism.

Rev Densil K Wright

Birth
21 Mar 1949
Death
23 Jun 2018
Burial
Pleasant Cemetery
Mount Sterling,
Madison County, Ohio

Densil worked in the drilling industry from 17 years of age until his death. He honorably served his country during the Vietnam War in the United States Army. He was a member of the South Columbus Freewill Baptist Church from 1973-1988 where he was also a deacon. In 1978 God called Densil to preach and in 1988 God moved him to the Mt. Sterling Freewill Baptist Church, first as an assistant pastor and then in 1989 he became pastor and served in that capacity until God called him home. Funeral Service with Rev. J.D. Bowman, officiating at the Mt. Sterling Freewill Baptist Church.

Nathaniel Wyatt

Birth:
Jan. 5, 1762
New York
Death:
Aug. 18, 1824
Norton
Delaware County
Ohio
Burial:
Wyatt Cemetery
Waldo
Marion County
Ohio

He was the son of Nathaniel Wyatt and Temperance Hubbell Wyatt. As a young man, Nathaniel Wyatt served in the Revolutionary War, in the New York Militia.

Nathaniel WYATT married Anna BRUNDIGE on October 1, 1786, in Ulster County, New York. Nathaniel and Anna Brundige WYATT started their married life in New York. From there, they migrated to Virginia. From Virginia, they settled briefly in Pickaway County, Ohio, and then settled in what was known as Marlborough Township, Delaware County, Ohio.

The Wyatt and Brundige families became known as the very first settlers in this area, upon their arrival there in February 1806.

Upon his homestead property, Nathaniel WYATT built, owned, and operated

Wyatt's Tavern & Hotel, which was a two-story brick building that served an important role in the history of this area of Ohio. Wyatt's Tavern & Hotel was located near the historic Military Road.

Wyatt's Tavern & Hotel was located within the protective stockade fort walls of historic Fort Morrow, all located on Nathaniel Wyatt's homestead property. Fort Morrow had a vital role in the military history of Ohio during the War of 1812 time period.

In addition to Wyatt's Tavern & Hotel, Nathaniel WYATT owned and operated an important mill business for many years in this area of Ohio. He is also noted in Marion County history books as serving as Justice of the Peace.

From his homestead, Nathaniel WYATT donated the land for the Wyatt Family Cemetery, which is the oldest cemetery in Marion County, Ohio. This cemetery is located near the original site of Wyatt's Tavern & Hotel and the historic site of Fort Morrow.Historically known as "Wyatt's Graveyard", the Wyatt Family Cemetery is situated on a beautiful knoll about 30 feet high on the west bank of the Olentangy River. Past veterans from the Revolutionary War, the War of 1812, and the Civil War are buried there, along with many of earliest settlers from Marion County and Delaware County, Ohio.

Nathaniel WYATT died on his homestead. The DELAWARE PATRON newspaper published in Delaware, Delaware County, Ohio, carried the news of his death in their weekly issue printed on 19 August 1824, in the following words:

"DIED ~ At Norton, last evening, Nathaniel WYATT, Esquire, an AGED and RESPECTABLE citizen."

Nathaniel Wyatt's estate sale was held later that fall on 5 November 1824 at his residence located in Marlborough Township.

In the 21 October 1824 edition of the DELAWARE PATRON newspaper, an advertisement proclaiming the news of his estate auction was advertised in this way:

"NATHANIEL WYATT's ESTATE ~ The personal property of said estate will be sold at public auction at the house of Nathaniel WYATT, deceased, in Marlborough Township, on the 5th day of November next (Year: 1824). Sale to commence at 10 o'clock on said day. Terms of sale made known at day of sale."

Nathaniel WYATT (1762 - 1824) was buried in historic Wyatt Cemetery in August 1824 where he rests today with many members of the Wyatt and Brundige families who played such a vital part in the early history and settlement of Delaware County and Marion County, Ohio.

Rev Samuel Wyatt
Birth:
Oct. 8, 1796
Death:
Aug. 25, 1842
Burial:
Wyatt Cemetery
Waldo
Marion County
Ohio

A Freewill Baptist minister, ordained 1827, mentored by Rev. David Dudley, and affiliated with the Mt. Pleasant church.

Rev John W. Wynn
Birth:
1857
Death:
1929
South Dakota
Burial:
Camden Cemetery
Kipton
Lorain County
Ohio
Plot: Section A - 31 West

News Topic: WYNN, JOHN W. Topic Details: Died In S. Dakota, Buried In Kipton;

Brief Obituary. Date: June 27, 1929. Source: Oberlin News Page: 1, Col: 6

He was on the 37th session program in 1907 Central Ohio Yearly Meeting at the west Mansfield FWB Church. He preached on Friday evening on Missions.

Gilbert Lafayette Yeley
Birth:
Nov. 2, 1868
Death:
Mar. 1, 1951
Scioto County,
Ohio
Burial:
Turner Cemetery
Scioto County,
Ohio

He was an early Free Will Baptist preacher in southern Ohio and represents a name that had many other notable Free Will Baptists.

He was farmer and filled pulpits as a Free Will Baptist minister. He was a member of Bloom FWB church. He married Mary Henning in 1890. His sister Miss Bessie Yeley was a missionary.

Bessie N. Yeley
Birth:
Nov. 26, 1895
Death:
Jan. 23, 1969

Wheelersburg,
Scioto County, Ohio
Burial:
Memorial Burial Park,
Wheelersburg,
Scioto County, Ohio

She was ordained by the Porter Conference of Free Will Baptists. In 1936, at the age of 40, Bessie entered Venezuela as a missionary. In subsequent years Bessie served in Cuba under Free Will Baptist Foreign Missions. She also served under the Home Mission Board in Arizona and Texas along the Mexican border, and later in Miami to Cuban refugees. She was ordained by the Porter Conference.

John Sowers Yeley
Birth:
Feb. 11, 1874
Slocum,
Scioto County, Ohio
Death:
Dec. 26, 1936
Scioto County, Ohio
Burial:
Vernon Cemetery, Lyra,
Scioto County, Ohio

Rev. Yeley began his career as a minister of the gospel at age 31 and continued in the service of Free Will Baptists for 25 years. He was a brother to missionary Bessie Yeley, who at the time of his death was serving as a missionary in Venezuela but later in Panama and Cuba. Many notable Free Will Baptists came from the Yeley family in the future years.

Benjamin Franklin Zell
Birth:
August 7, 1833
Warren County, Ohio
Death:
1916
Burial:
Miami Cemetery
Corwin
Warren County,
Ohio

He was educated at Mainville Academy and Lebanon normal school. He was ordained in 1862 by Elder Cyrus Dudley, John Hisey and F. Myers. In 1856 he was married to Jane M. Phillips. In 1863 he moved to Salem, Indiana and took charge of the Salem, Ridgeville, and Bear Creek churches. The following year he returned to Ohio and assumed the pastorates of the East Liberty, Union, York, Green, and Newton churches. With these churches he labored 14 years. During that time he baptized over 600 persons.. He was on the 37th session program in 1907 Central Ohio Yearly Meeting at the west Mansfield FWB Church. He led in the Y M Covenant meeting.

Zell, Rev. B. F., son of John and Mary (Tyson) Zell, was born in Warren County, O., Aug. 7, 1833. He was educated at Mainville Academy and Lebanon Normal School. He was ordained in 1862 by Elder Cyrus Dudley, John Hisey and F. Myers. In 1856 he was married to Jane M. Phillips, and has three children. In 1863 he moved to Salem, Ind., and took charge of the Salem, Ridgeville, and Bear Creek churches. The following year he returned to Ohio, and assumed the pastorate of the East Liberty, Union, York and Newton churches. With these churches he labored fourteen years. During that time he baptized and received into the churches over six hundred persons. Three new meeting-houses were built, and one church was organized. Since then he has preached for the La Rue, Green Camp, Pleasant Grove, and Grand Prairie churches. He has served the Ohio, and the Ohio Central Y. M's as clerk, and has been three times a delegate to the General Conference. He is at present pastor of the La Rue and Grand Prairie churches.

Death Has No Strength; Jesus Has Subdued Its Power